ESSAYS IN COMPARATIVE EDUCATION

Education and the Economy

Education and the Economy

General Editor

Joseph A. Lauwerys, D.Sc., D.Lit., F.R.I.C.
Professor of Comparative Education in the University of London

 Evans Brothers Limited London

Published by
Evans Brothers Limited
Montague House
Russell Square
London WC1

Printed in Great Britain in 12 point Bembo by
Cox & Wyman Ltd., London, Fakenham and Reading

CSD 237 35115 3   PR 4831
PB 237 35122 3

Contents

The Contributors
C. Arnold Anderson, Director, Comparative Education Center, University of Chicago; George Z. F. Bereday, Professor of Comparative Education, Teachers College, Columbia University; Mary Jean Bowman, Research Associate Professor, Department of Economics and Comparative Education Center, University of Chicago; Mark Blaug, Professor of Economics of Education, University of London Institute of Education; Brian Holmes, Reader in Comparative Education in the University of London; Laura Goodman Howe, formerly Assistant Editor, World Year Book of Education; Robert King Hall, formerly Professor of Education, Teachers College, Columbia University; Joseph A. Lauwerys, Professor of Comparative Education in the University of London.

Preface

In 1948 the Editorial Board of the *Year Book of Education* decided that each volume would deal, from a world-wide point of view, with one large theme, topic or problem such as, for example, 'the roles and functions of teachers' or 'social mobility and education'. The first post-war volume, under the editorship of Dr. Nicholas Hans and myself, dealt with the effects of war upon education.

Since then, each *Year Book* has had as an Introduction a long essay in which an attempt has been made to extract from the various contributions presented such general conclusions as seemed possible. These essays are thus a kind of synthesis indicating common concerns and world-wide trends of change. Since the problems analysed are deep and complex – some are perennial – the editorial introductions are, in many cases, entirely relevant to present-day situations.

But most *Year Books* are out of print and not every library possesses copies. Moreover, interest in Comparative Education has grown enormously. It is now very widely taught in universities and colleges of education. It was therefore thought useful to reprint the essays in a form that would make them accessible to students. Those presented in this first volume are concerned with the influence of religion and ideology upon education. I hope readers will enjoy them and that they will be encouraged to turn their attention to the *Year Books* themselves. They will find there articles and contributions of fascinating interest, as fresh and lively now as they were when first printed.

J. A. LAUWERYS

Education and the Transformation of Societies

from the 1954 Year Book of Education
Robert King Hall
Joseph A. Lauwerys

A great economic revolution is sweeping across the world and a new climate of thought and feeling is being created. Characteristic of it, especially in the new nations of Asia and Africa, is a naïve and optimistic faith in the power of education. Many believe that in the societies of tomorrow the school will take the dominating place occupied in medieval cities by the cathedral: the centre and focus of the aspirations of the community, the agency through which the level of life is raised and ennobled. All this is no new thing. From Plato onwards, philosophers have given expression to such hopes. For centuries statesmen have paid at least lip-service to the same ideals. But now the great masses of the people have been fired by them and they have learned to see in the school an instrument by which their children may be given a chance to reach new heights.

The much publicized achievements in education of the Soviet Union and of Japan have perhaps been decisive in spreading this outlook. Everybody knows that the U.S.S.R. has devoted an immense effort to the elimination of illiteracy, to the diffusion of technical knowledge, and to the strengthening of political loyalty. It is well realized that success here was the necessary condition for success in the industrial and, ultimately, in the military fields. Japan, too, was at once the most literate, the most industrialized, and the most powerful nation of Asia. The advanced countries of the West know, and have known for years, that here, in the area of education, is the very heart of the whole problem of satisfying the wishes of their less fortunate neighbours. An illustration is the support given, right from the start, to Unesco's efforts in 'Fundamental Education'. 'That is a subject which interests a large number of our member states,' said the first Executive Secretary of the Organization; 'we are really going to turn into action the provisions that have been made about removing poverty and ignorance and helping the poorer sections of the world community.'

In addition, internal political conditions since the end of World War II have everywhere favoured the ready acceptance of these views. In the West, the parties which represent the interests of organized workers, have pressed continuously for easier access to secondary schools and universities, thereby affirming their belief that more education for all is a good thing. In Asia and Africa, nations having attained full political independence are turning to the next part of their historic task: the achievement of full social and economic independence. Their leaders have well understood that the condition for this is the mobilization not only of natural but of human resources, and that schools can be used to this end. Thus, one of the first decisions of the new government of the Indian Union in 1946 was that a fifty-year development plan for education should be put through in fifteen years. Similarly, as soon as the government of the Gold Coast obtained effective power over internal affairs, it decided to introduce compulsory education for all children at once, disregarding completely such difficulties as shortages of teachers and of buildings.

The tide continues to run strongly. Yet, listening to the discussions of experts, a certain touch of disappointment and anxiety is noticed. Mass-education campaigns have not been as successful as had been hoped and the results are not always what had been expected. In some regions there is a flagging of effort, and scepticism is often expressed. There is a growing realization that the problem of achieving social transformation and economic betterment through education has not been fully understood in all its terrifying complexity. It is becoming clear that even if education is necessary to progress, it is not by itself sufficient. It can exercise its beneficent effects only if factories, as well as schools, are built, if production methods are changed, if new social institutions develop. Furthermore, not every kind of schooling is useful. Merely to copy the education of the West may be not only futile but positively harmful. The task of translating European methods into another social idiom, of adapting them to a new climate, is more complicated and difficult than was once thought. There is need for an educational theory capable of adequately directing practical effort. One aim of the 1954 *Year Book* was to make a contribution to the diagnosis and analysis which must be the foundation of such a theory.

Let us look first at the under-developed regions. By this term we do not imply that these are backward in culture, humanity, or civilization, but only that their populations have not yet learned to use fully the powers which science and technology have created. In this broader sense under-developed areas are found even in the most fully industrialized countries, for example in the Highlands of Scotland and the mountains of Tennessee. Evidently, such regions display great diversity of structure and a wide range of religious, cultural, and linguistic characteristics. They have in common, how-ever, a widespread desire to acquire the apparatus and the gadgets of a machine civilization. Everywhere people want television sets, motor-cars, and refrigerators. But for the most part they have no desire for the patterns of thought and behaviour typical of those national groups which have created modern science and twentieth-century industrialism. Europeans do not wish to ape Americans: and Asians do not for the most part want to shed their traditional culture. They seem to have but small appetite for industrial discipline and Western mores. What they seek is the external result, the fruit without the preliminary preparation and labour.

Two questions arise imperiously: Is Western technology detach-able from the Western cultural ground? Is it transferable to anyone who learn the technical tricks? Natives born in central African villages can certainly learn these simple techniques and a few may qualify as engineers and scientists. Yet this does not take us far. To learn to drive a tractor is easy. To learn how to maintain its produc-tive performance and how to repair it is another matter, for it is not a one-man skill. And to learn how to design, produce, and finance the distribution of this tractor is a still more difficult problem. To make and to maintain large numbers of complicated machines requires a deep change in a whole community. The examples of the Soviet

Union and of Japan seem to negate this view – but there were special historical factors in each case. Western Russia in 1918 had already reached a considerable degree of industrial development and it was, without doubt, part of the European complex. It possessed excellent universities and technical colleges. The tasks of the Soviet leaders have been, then, first to diffuse knowledge and skill among the masses– a problem similar to that found in all other European countries – and next to transmit Western culture from the European three-quarters to the Asian quarter. As for Japan, that country had in 1870 a homogeneous, well-disciplined, obedient, and industrious people; a relatively small area with easy communications; pride in the past and faith in the future; a culture pattern not in any way antagonistic to modern industrial organization; and above all far-sighted leadership of much political wisdom. The situation here was unique. Besides, the social techniques employed were extremely ruthless and affected every aspect of everyone's life. They would be unacceptable to any human group that has been touched by humanitarian and liberal ideals or which pays attention to individual rights and freedoms.

Yet another instance of the successful adoption of industrial civilization is Europe itself. Six hundred years ago that sub-continent was neither technically nor scientifically ahead of China, India, or the Muslim world. The expectation of life of its inhabitants was no greater, their social institutions no more developed, their philosophy no more subtle, their habitual modes of thought no less superstitious. Europe, however, was favoured by a set of very special circumstances: in the first place by the discovery of the Americas, which put a premium upon science and gave it high prestige while at the same time placing in the hands of enterprising and vigorous groups unlimited resources of land and capital. The 'high' intellectual traditions developed in its universities favoured the growth of a positive science which in the hands of men of genius like Galileo taught how best to exploit natural resources. New social institutions were invented and established and they promoted commercial and industrial initiative. Its mores strengthened a respect for individual liberties which, in turn, released a great fund of invention and energy. Western Europe created industrial technology and, in the course of centuries, absorbed it into its social structure and way of life. It was a native growth: the problem faced was one of cultural development, not one of the assimilation of foreign elements. Of course Europe learned from other areas. The imports from Asia and from the Americas changed the diet and the habits of all. Eastern art and African rhythms modified aesthetic standards. Devices like the Chinese system of civil service examinations were adopted. But all this was, in a sense, little more than superficial adaptation. It was not a massive adoption of a whole technology. At no stage was there anything like a challenge to fundamental values, nor was there a demand for radical changes in patterns of thought, attitude, and behaviour. And Europe had time for a gradual and evolutionary change. Modern under-developed nations are starting late, entering a highly competitive modern world when technology is far advanced and enormously more complex. Their very survival in fact depends upon a rapid, almost revolutionary, adjustment to these new demands on society.

Cultural Transmission

Whenever different cultures have made contact they have learned from each other. The process of imitation and borrowing is one of the dominant themes in the history of mankind. It is recorded in the memoirs of generals, in the archives of trading companies, in the files of modern cartels. It appears in the sacred writings of the great world religions and on the stone monuments scattered across six thousand years of history in the Middle East. In all these historical data the instruments and techniques of transmission – as well as the motives of those who gave and of those who received – are clearly perceived.

The oldest method of transmitting technical knowledge was simply by demonstration and imitation. It was thus that the great fundamental inventions of fire, of agriculture, of domestication of animals, of use of metals, gradually diffused across the world. Even today it continues. The housewife who tells her neighbour how she cooks a particularly delicious dish; the county agent who shows his friends the latest findings of the great agricultural experimental stations; and the surgeon at a medical conference who describes his successful operations, are all using this ancient process.

Trade, commerce, and industry have played a part of fundamental importance. There have been few instruments of technological transmission more effective than the great British and Dutch East

Indies trading companies. Italian caravans to Cathay left a track of European and Near Eastern influence across Central Asia that can still be seen. And in modern times the place of these mercantile ventures has been taken by the great plantations and the petroleum companies penetrating into remote deserts and jungles; by international airlines and European-constructed railways; by hydro-electric power stations and a complex of manufacturing subsidiaries; by mass merchandizing organizations, radio advertising, and foreign brand names. Even languages have changed under this impact – and *colt* means revolver, *kodak* means camera, *portland* means cement, and *coke* a soft drink. Silk mills from Lyons, cotton mills from Manchester, steel mills from Pittsburgh, and pharmaceutical plants from every major Western power are operating under local management, with local labour, for local profit, in half the under-developed areas of the world. The educational effects of this enormous diffusion process have been incalculable, perhaps the largest of all in terms of persons reached and degree of social change produced.

Great journeys, however, have not been undertaken only by those who wanted to buy and sell. There have been pilgrimages to sacred places and wanderings of missionaries driven by faith. These felt that they had to carry a light to their less fortunate brethren and teach them higher values and better ways. The monks who moved northwards into Europe after the downfall of the Roman Empire taught Christian beliefs and morality to the Barbarians and preserved in their monasteries the technical knowledge as well as the philosophy of the Classical world. And in modern times missionaries have transmitted to the native peoples of Africa, Asia, and America the science, technology, and ethics of the West.

The spread of a world religion is always accompanied by the spread of knowledge of certain sacred books and thus of a language and of a writing-system. The Latin and Greek alphabets are used wherever Christianity has been established. The Arabic alphabet has followed the Koran. When the King of Kudara, one of the ancient principalities of Korea, sent his envoy Achiki to the court of Emperor Ōjin of Japan in A.D. 285 he was accompanied by Wani, a tutor for the Emperor's son. Among his teaching materials were the *Analects* of Confucius and the *Thousand Ideographs*. Wani came to the Kyoto court to instruct the Crown Prince in the Chinese art of writing, but he did more than introduce an ideographic system into Japan: he also brought Confucian philosophy, which converted the majority of the people to a new religion, changed fundamentally indigenous Japanese art and architecture, and profoundly influenced the philosophy, social system, and politics of the Japanese people from that time to this.

In this connexion, mention might also be made of Kemal Atatürk's famed 1928 reform of the Turkish alphabet which ostensibly aimed at increasing the efficiency of Turkish communications and at assisting the growth of literacy among the masses. Actually it turned out to be one of the most effective political and educational devices ever adopted to draw a curtain between a people and its past. It functioned as a screen through which the culture of the past had to pass in order to reach the generations of the future. Only those old books which were thought to advance the political goals of the Turkish Revolution were transliterated to the new script, and to those who were educated after 1928 the old books were as incomprehensible as if written in some unknown foreign language.

Empires and Colonies

Not only trade and religion, but war and conquest help to transmit knowledge and skill. The impact of armies on civil populations may itself be educative – the Roman legions in Romania and the Normans in England, to mention only far-distant episodes. In modern times, the whole idea of empire-building has fallen into disrepute and the name 'imperialist' has become a term of abuse. Yet the contributions made by great empires to the advancement of mankind is immense. They established peace over vast areas and thereby facilitated the movement of men, goods, and ideas; they spread better seeds, new plants, and improved techniques. Rome taught its subject peoples engineering, military science, and law, while better methods of husbandry spread all over the Mediterreanean basin and even beyond. Its influence can be seen today not only in the ruins of Palmyra and Petra but in the laws of Argentina and Portugal; in the organization of the Catholic Church and the Latin alphabet. When the English Raj withdrew from India, a legacy of unifying language remained, as well as more than four hundred institutions of higher learning, and a civil service pre-eminent in the world. And Indians, whatever their mother tongue may be, continue to make contact with the West through the medium of English, their *lingua franca*. The Spanish Empire virtually obliterated three great civilizations but left a continent and a half indelibly stamped with Spanish culture, and through it, with Roman, Greek, and Muslim cultures. Marching up the black stone balustrades of Persepolis are the bas-relief figures of colonial peoples from the Empire of Darius, bringing their offerings of goods and services, pooling the technological knowledge of their time. And on the walls of the temples of Luxor and Karnak, in the tombs of the Valley of the Kings, there are the hieroglyphic records of the contribution of subject peoples to the rulers of the Upper Nile. Often the defeated peoples were reduced to slavery, a degrading and brutalizing thing both for conqueror and conquered. Yet, in drawing up a balance sheet, the gains should not be overlooked. In the ninety years since Emancipation the descendants of slaves in the United States have moved from abject poverty to the second most favoured economic position in the world today, excelled only by the white population of the United States[1]. American Negroes enjoy a higher average annual income than any European population, they have a larger proportion of university graduates and have access to those higher professional posts which in other countries are the preserve of the upper classes. Brazil offers an equally impressive example, in the creation of a new race and a new culture through the miscegenation of the Portuguese ruling groups with emancipated Negro slaves.

The Changing Role of Government

On the whole, knowledge of new techniques tended to diffuse rather slowly in the past: it took nearly two thousand years for the Gauls to learn from the Egyptians how to smelt iron, and the potato was not consumed in large quantities in Europe before the middle of the eighteenth century – nearly two hundred years after its first introduction. As time went on, however, and as civilization advanced, things moved more quickly. In the first place, communications became speedier and printing facilitated quick diffusion of learning. In the second place, governments themselves, as they assumed greater responsibilities, began to take interest in training the populations they

---

[1] Leaving out of account the curious case of the Sheikdom of Kuwait, where oil royalties give its semi-nomadic population a *per capita* income twice that of the United States.

ruled so as to increase their productivity and thus their capacity to pay taxes. The British rulers of India, for example, encouraged the building of schools and the education of a class capable of providing clerks and civil servants. In a word, they set themselves deliberately to transform – at least in certain aspects – the cultural patterns of dependent populations, using education for that end.

Education is, of course, itself an aspect of cultural transmission. Everywhere and always it has been the agency through which the culture of the present generation is transmitted to or, better, recreated in the next. The pattern of colonial education, however, was something else. Provided for adults, it was an agency for adding on to an existing culture certain elements drawn from another. Provided for young people, it was an attempt to form them into one culture – usually the Western – while all out-of-school influences fostered the growth of another. Inevitably, the results were often very different from those aimed at. Nevertheless they were impressive enough and they catalysed social change.

One effect of such policies has been that in every country which is or was once a colony or a semi-independent protectorate there is now a numerous class of intelligent men, who are well acquainted with Western thought but whose emotional and cultural roots lie elsewhere. These – they are often called the *intelligentsia* – are the groups which have led their countries to political independence and who are now shaping their future.

It should be noted that what has been said above applies particularly to colonial powers like Britain, France or Belgium. But when other nations, such as the United States, developed industry and reached out for markets and for sources of raw materials, they too became interested in transmitting certain aspects of their culture. Since, for a variety of reasons, they did not rule over colonial domains their effort was channelled chiefly into the activities of independent commercial enterprises or specialized agencies of international organizations.

In modern times, international clubs and associations, such as Rotary International, International Chamber of Commerce, and the Masonic Lodge, conduct major educational programmes. International labour unions and professional associations are media of exchange of technical information. Organizations like the International Air Transport Association link major industries in many parts of the world, establish international standards of operational techniques, and maintain minimum levels of training for their members' staffs. Great philanthropic foundations, like the Rockefeller Foundation, Carnegie Corporation, Kellogg Foundation, and Ford Foundation, carry on very extensive international programmes of education, and exchange of technical information and personnel. In recent years, there has grown up an impressive list of governmental and international organizations designed to provide similar services: the Pan-American Union, the Institute of Inter-American Affairs, The British Council and the *Alliance Française*, the United States Information Service, the Institute of International Education, and Unesco.

The development of international as opposed to national agencies is, on the whole, welcomed by the governments of under-developed countries. Most are intensely jealous of their national independence and not only suspicious but resentful of anything that might be interpreted as economic imperialism, but they realize only too well the difficulties of their task and their own need of help, both material and technological. Aid extended by any single country is open to objections which are not raised acutely when it is provided through the agency of an organization partly under the control of the recipient.

The great cry, of course, is for speed and yet more speed. The example of Japan has been quoted continually. Here was a country which had emerged in twenty-five years from a medieval feudalism to a modern state capable of decisively defeating China, then the greatest nation in Asia. In another ten years it had humbled Tsarist Russia, one of Europe's major powers, and presented the world with the reality of Asia's first technological state. Twelve years later Japan was able to dictate terms to the victorious Allies and win an empire in the Pacific. Fourteen years later it had the third greatest navy and defied the world as it marched into continental Asia. And by 1941, only ninety-three years after emerging from the chrysalis of the medieval Tokugawa Shogunate, Japan was one of the seven Great Powers of the world, and for two years fought the Allies to a standstill in the Pacific.

After World War II, in view of such achievements, the spokesmen for the under-developed territories demanded the fruits of Western technological skill. They rejected evolutionary change, and cried out for immediate revolutionary social improvement. They charged that their progress had been grossly delayed by the exploitation of imperial governments and avaricious private industry. The possibility that the soil for technological development had in their instance not been receptive, and that the seeds which had been planted had failed to germinate, was summarily dismissed as European rationalization and imperialist propaganda.

The Reaction of the West

These claims did not affect the U.S.S.R. in any immediate way, apart from opening up possibilities of propaganda and of political activity. The Soviet Union had suffered much damage during the war and an enormous task of reconstruction had to be tackled. In consequence, for some years there was little surplus left to assist in the industrial development of Eastern European states: a fact which may have helped to bring about the break with Yugoslavia, an under-developed country eager to adopt modern methods of manufacture. But the Soviet Union undoubtedly continued, perhaps with increased zeal, the pre-war policy of fostering the economic and industrial growth of its own backward Asiatic republics. The whole of this area being closely controlled and guarded, there is little information available regarding what has been happening, and it is difficult to judge the part that education is called upon to play or the degree of success that has been achieved.

From the point of view of the West, however, the situation was a revolutionary one. A wave of intense nationalist feeling was sweeping across all the less industrialized countries. It was clear that these were absolutely determined to take their fate into their own hands, no matter what the cost. India, Pakistan, Burma, Indonesia attained political independence. In some countries, the property of foreign companies was seized without compensation, in others the mere proposal to accept loans from abroad in order to develop oil fields led to riots in the streets. It seemed to Western observers as though some people would prefer to allow natural resources to lie idle under the soil or oil to run into the sea rather than to let foreigners profit from turning such raw material into wealth for all. The overwhelming fear, of course, was that these same foreigners would exercise too much political pressure upon the national government and claim special privileges.

Such a dilemma is, in fact, tragic. On the one hand, there was a clamour for a quick rise in the standard of living, a rise possible only if very large investments, representing capital goods, could be secured from abroad. On the other hand, there was the destruction of those social and political conditions which encourage either private persons or governments to take the risks attendant upon foreign investment.

Furthermore, countries like France and Great Britain, with a long tradition of lending capital, are no longer in a position to meet the needs fully. France has been bled white by a long and rapacious occupation, and is much stretched by a continuing effort to reconstruct the French Union on a new political basis. Nevertheless, since 1948 to the time of writing France spent a greater proportion of her national income than any other nation on the development of her overseas territories. The United Kingdom has done whatever her resources allowed, of course, chiefly in relation to countries within the British Commonwealth of Nations. Debts to the new Asian dominions and to the Middle East have been paid largely in capital goods. Loans were made to the African territories and the Colonial Development Fund was greatly expanded. Attempts were made by the government itself, at great cost, to develop new forms of agricultural production, for example that of ground-nuts in Kenya and Tanganyika and of poultry in Gambia. These attempts tragically failed, partly for technical and partly for social reasons, though valuable lessons were expensively learned. Lastly, many of these measures were consolidated in the Colombo Plan. The total effort was vast. The total contribution in 1954, in gifts and loans to underdeveloped countries, exceeded £450 millions – about $1·25 billions.

The United States also reacted strongly to the world situation – usually in a way which, far from excluding nations which, like Sweden or Switzerland, controlled no colonies, encouraged their participation in the industrialization of under-developed countries. There were measures of relief like UNRRA and all sorts of activities promoted by the United Nations; to all of which the U.S.A. contributed generously. True to her faith in private enterprise the United States Government also tried to encourage investment abroad, but American finance proved in this field to be rather cautious and conservative. This is easy to understand: experience certainly did not encourage the taking of genuine risks and, besides, there were plenty of rewarding opportunities in the domestic field. The gap was filled to some extent by grants and gifts of astonishing generosity but, by 1949, it had become clear that even more was needed. President Truman then stated what has come to be known as the 'Point Four Policy' in his Inaugural Address of January 20th, 1949, entitled *The Faith of the American People*. He held that although there were limits to what the U.S.A. could afford to do for the assistance of other nations, 'imponderable resources in technical knowledge are constantly growing and are inexhaustible'. He called upon his countrymen to 'embark on a bold new programme for making the benefits of our scientific advances and industrial progress available for the improvement and growth of under-developed areas'. A few reflections on the Point Four Policy might be appropriate here.

President Truman's statement aroused exaggerated hopes. The astonishing growth in the industrial production of the U.S.A. and the prosperity of its inhabitants was known in the most remote parts of the world. It was the Mecca of engineers and the Utopia of technologists. Evidently, the fantastic output of the country was the outcome of a fortunate interaction between two sets of factors: a new continent rich in raw materials and a society capable of exploiting them and putting them to use. Americans themselves are sometimes prone to play down the importance of the first – the wealth of natural resources – and to stress the qualities of their fellow citizens: their drive, energy, and technical 'know-how'. Many of them tend to believe that the world's material problems could easily be solved if only other nations could acquire these industrial virtues and learn the technological 'know-how'. Thus President Truman's proposal was often seen as a problem of teaching. In his contribution to the 1954 *Year Book*, Dr. Paul Duncan wrote that 'In its application Point Four has been essentially a gigantic effort in mass education . . . in earning a living, in maintaining health, in raising a family, in contributing to community and national life . . . self-help is the keynote. Nevertheless, as Dr. Duncan points out, it was hoped also to 'foster capital investment in areas needing development', and this for the good of those areas. 'The old imperialism – exploitation for foreign profits – has no place in our plans.'

In spite of these reassurances and of the undoubted benefits that have already been brought to many countries, criticism has been harsh. In part this is simply the result of disillusionment. Many nations submitted grandiose plans which would have entailed expenditure as large as the total which the United States Congress was willing to authorize for aid to all the world. Some recipients felt humiliated by what they considered insignificant allotments, while others resented controls over the use of the funds. The social results of economic projects appeared unduly delayed. Foreign advisers and recipient nations differed in their basic philosophy regarding the ways the funds should be spent, and there followed the inevitable friction between proud peoples of basically different backgrounds.

Foreign criticism of the Point Four, and of subsequent American Technical Assistance programmes, has been of four types. Confirmed Marxists have argued against it on the ground that their philosophy showed that it must have degrading and anti-democratic effects. Those who are committed to antagonistic political ideologies (whether of the extreme Right or Left), as well as many moderates who are rather cynical of the motives of the Great Powers, have argued that capitalism is not and cannot be idealistic and that what is proposed as philanthropy is actually a disguised attempt to secure foreign markets and controls. Some leaders in under-developed countries, representing powerful and sometimes corrupt vested interests, tended to look upon the programme as a 'pork barrel', and to demand increased aid. They maintained that the United States *owes* them more help, and threatened co-operation with Communism if that aid were not forthcoming. Finally, Point Four has been seriously criticized by honest and well-meaning people who have been unwilling to recognize the social costs which they must pay if the programme is to succeed. They welcome and expect its material benefits. But they fear the economic, social, and political changes entailed.

Criticism of the programme has not been limited to foreign observers and recipient nations. There has been a strong and vocal opposition to the policy within the United States. Most Americans have been willing to grant the weight of many of the arguments which President Truman advanced to justify his proposal. There is a powerful factor of humanitarianism in American society, and an uncomfortable feeling is experienced when it is realized that the United States has half the industrial wealth of the world while two-thirds of the world's population lives in misery. The American points with pride to fifty-four philanthropic foundations which in 1953 had $1,000,000 to $450,000,000 each in assets; and welcomes the more than thirty thousand foreign students who each year study in the United States – more than 60 per cent of them from under-developed areas. Many, indeed, accept the basic political theses – that the United States has a moral obligation and will build up a reservoir of goodwill by meeting it; that the nation itself will ultimately benefit economically by building up markets for high-priced goods; and that it will benefit strategically by opposing communism with strong and economically healthy regimes. Yet many Americans experience certain doubts.

There is, in the first place, a relatively small minority of traditiona isolationists, who contend that interference in foreign affairs is none of America's business. There is a larger group which sincerely wants to help the peoples of the depressed areas, but fears that help through existing channels will merely perpetuate what seem to them bad political regimes and undesirable social classes. They fear that the United States will become identified with the regimes they deal with and will thus be discredited in the eyes of the world. But by far the largest percentages of the critics reject the methods rather than the goals of the policy. They hold that governmental assistance cannot be economically successful where an ordinary commercial venture would not be. They hold that government underwriting is bad strategically because it involves the United States in political risks and may lead to war. They believe this to be nothing but 'neo-colonialism'.

Lessons Learned

Yet in spite of these criticisms and doubts, technical-assistance pro-grammes have gone on developing and are gathering momentum

By now an enormous amount of experience has been gathered by the old 'Colonial Powers', such as Britain and France, as well as by relative newcomers like the United States. In particular, certain doubts become stronger as prospects progress to the point where results can be appraised.

To begin with, there is the question of whether education and technical assistance are properly used if the result is merely to improve degree rather than to change kind. For instance, it has been held that if a peasant in an under-developed area can learn to increase his yield by only a very small amount it will enormously improve his living standard. This humanitarian and charitable view led to the policy known as technical assistance at the 'grass roots' – teaching how to read, to raise a few more bushels to the acres, produce a better egg or build a better 'privy' – the sort of thing aimed at in the early days of 'Fundamental Education' or 'Mass Education'. It is now generally recognized that small uniform increases of income, without major capital accumulations, are simply swallowed up and have no measurable impact upon the standard of living of a people. A great part of the world's population lives in backward economic systems which are anachronistic and which, regardless of increased productivity through improved techniques, can never support a modern living standard. The problem, then, seems to be one of selective development in depth, permitting one section of the population or one geographical area to make major advances through a fundamental change in the technology and economy, and thus to jump beyond the subsistence level so as to be able to accumulate capital. The choice of which group or area to favour, in view of the impossibility of equal and simultaneous improvement for all, may involve a politically difficult and emotionally bitter decision. But the alternative has proved to be inadequate.

Connected with this is a major doubt as to the relevance of the definition of 'standard of living' adopted by the United Nations and others: indeed one wonders whether the concept itself is helpful or even meaningful. The whole idea is based on a materialistic appraisal of Western society and upon a money economy. This view is sustained by the official definition of an under-developed area as being that in which the annual income is below $400 a head. But how is 'standard of living' to be measured? One thinks first of better health, greater personal freedom, higher levels of education and of cultural appreciation, more goods in the shops. Are all these simply to be measured in cash? Obviously not. And it is useless to increase the wealth of a country if there is neither political freedom nor cultural opportunity in which to enjoy the fruits of material advance. In fact, here is a contradiction: can 'a better life' be promoted if intervention in the cultural and political patterns is precluded?

In any case, what is meant by 'a better life'? Shall it be modelled on the antiseptic, efficient, dynamic, moneyed, and phrenetic culture pattern of the technological West? Or shall it be the contemplative, leisurely, mystical, class-structured, traditional society of the under-developed area? As we have pointed out earlier, the vocal leader of a depressed population may want the motorcars, refrigerators, and higher purchasing power that comes with the machine and modern technology. But he may be reluctant to relinquish his ancient ways – his village system, the status of his women, his hordes of servants, his religious observances, his political vested interests. He does not realize that the machine brings with it the set of moral and ethical commitments from which the invention sprang. Western technology *can* give better medicine, but the improved health conditions will bring in their train lower infant mortality, higher birth-rates, increased population, demographic pressure, and, ultimately, social readjustment to meet this new cultural problem. The recipient society cannot avoid the problem: it can only select from a choice of possible solutions – slums, low-cost housing, altered wage structures, changed economics, immigration, birth control, mystical withdrawal from reality, destruction of family systems and increased mechanization.

The greatest lesson learned from post-war experience, then, is that it is easier to establish modern industrial technology than to solve the social, moral and ethical problems that ensue. Any competent technician can plan a steel mill in India or establish a rubber plantation in Malaya. There are no instructional problems in preparing Saudi Arabian *bedouins* or the African *bantus* for jobs in a Western technical enterprise, which any competent educator working with a plant superintendent and foreman cannot easily resolve. Production and instruction are surprisingly easy, and the world's successful experience is enormous. But neither production nor instruction inevitably lead to a solution of the real problems: the moral choices which will transform technological procedures into a real and desired improvement in the standard of living. It is to a solution of these ethical problems that the West must turn if the process of technical assistance is not to fail miserably and the effort be discredited. When Leo Tolstoy, who as a youth had led a life both varied and wild, started teaching, he asked himself the question: what moral right have I, an adult, to train children to follow my example and to mould their flexible minds in my own image? He answered in the negative and gave his pupils full freedom to decide for themselves what to do. And, later, he abandoned teaching because he was not able consistently to follow his own principles. The parable has its point. Are we of the West certain that what is good for us is good for all? What in our way of life is good intrinsically, good in itself? What can we safely pass on to other peoples without disrupting fundamentally the very bases of their lives? In relation to these questions, let us consider some problems of policy.

Policy Problems: Production

Technical and educational assistance to independent nations can be given only when it is desired by the recipient. But there is always the difficult problem of determining who shall speak for a people in expressing their desires. Is it to be the government, or a ruling clique, or a vested interest, or an uninformed mass? And in addition there will be the question of whether it is really possible for the masses of an under-developed area to make a choice: for can they reasonably know the consequences which will accrue from the introduction of technology? Leaving this issue on one side and assuming that assistance is to be given, note should be made that the donor agency – whatever its nature – has to consider difficult problems of production, distribution, control of resources, and control of personnel. Under the first of these headings, four decisions will have to be made.

First, is there any moral obligation to help what may become a competitor? In answering this question, the donor agency will, of course, begin by deciding whether the new possible competitor may not in fact become a better customer. Will the recipients create competitive, or rather ancillary, industries? Will the donor agency be able to invest funds and repatriate profits? If the answer to the first question is that the new economy will in fact be competitive in major areas, then a second question must be asked: is there in international technical assistance something ethically equivalent to 'fair competition' in a domestic economy? Where the donor agency is a private corporation instead of a national government, the question must be asked whether or not the monopolistic practices of an international cartel is an evil thing and whether there should be anti-trust agreements limiting such practices. Finally, the donor agency must ask if it is morally bound to extend aid even when the project is financially unremunerative. Must it provide capital, patents, and research data, technical training, and education? Must a foreign agency aid a depressed area for philanthropic reasons, when the political climate or the economic realities preclude the venture from becoming economically self-sufficient?

Second, the donor agency must decide who has the right and the obligation to determine which of several alternative plans for technological advancement shall be adopted. No major area presents a single, unchallenged, certain solution to its problem of developing its natural resources. Various vested-interest groups will present various proposals. Who shall decide between them? Does the donor agency have the right to dictate solutions? Is this outside agency technically competent to select the 'best solution' for an under-developed area? Does it have the right to control programmes in which it has invested money? Or is the donor agency merely a neutral technical consultant, somewhat akin to a library reference book?

The third policy decision with regard to production is whether the development shall be *vertical*, through self-sufficient and self-sustaining economic projects, or *horizontal*, through wide-scale, non-sustaining aid programmes. Among the detailed decisions which must be made in determining this policy will be that of choosing between a development programme organized for immediate production and one for future social and economic advancement. What type of industrial organization shall be used? What percentage of local labour used? Shall the industry be responsible for training personnel, or shall the general public? Shall the industry be organized to be self-sufficient, or dependent on local ancillary industries? Shall the wage structure be such as to encourage paternalism, or a system of free enterprise in the society?

The fourth, and one of the most difficult, policy problems will be that of determining who shall be chosen to receive the training. It is not enough to establish testing devices for technological aptitude. The real question is whether or not the donor agency, governmental or private, has the moral right to select the future *élite* of the area. An equally crucial and puzzling problem is that of determining who shall receive the capital or industrial contracts. Shall the choice be truly competitive or deliberately slanted to favour certain groups? Shall there be ethical prerequisites such as labour conditions, levels of profits, codes of business ethics, absence of monopoly practices, financial responsibility?

Policy Problems: Distribution

Little attention has usually been paid to the problem of equitable distribution. It has been assumed that increased productivity, the simple creation of more wealth, will inevitably benefit the general population regardless of existing systems of distribution. Obviously this is not the case, and many of the gains may be siphoned off into the pockets of certain privileged classes, or even exported from the country to be used abroad. Such a misuse of profits from a technical-assistance programme defeats its very purpose. The foreign donor agency has to face two critical questions of policy: How shall the increased production be divided? What support shall be given to undesirable cliques in the recipient regime?

The foreign donor of technical assistance must ask itself whether it has in fact any right of control over the use of the profits accruing from a technical-assistance project. Obviously, if it is a private industrial organization, it will have rights to that portion of the profit which is paid to it in return for its technical competence and the use of its funds. But the crucial issue arises in the use of the additional profits which are retained by the under-developed area and which are the *raison d'être* of the technical-assistance programme. If those benefits resulting from the programme are misused, or primarily benefit a part of the society which is unacceptable to the general public, the overseas agency will almost inevitably be stigmatized. Yet it must ask whether it really has the right to manipulate the domestic use of the increased production and whether it is obliged to deal only with local agencies which have an 'acceptable' ethical standard; who shall determine what is in fact an acceptable ethical standard; and finally if it is possible for an outside agency to control or basically influence domestic policy without infringing upon the sovereignty of the under-developed area.

The problem becomes of critical importance when the donor agency is the agency of a foreign government. Its actions may then lead to charges of imperialism or of 'dollar diplomacy'. Such an agency obviously does not have complete freedom in dealing with recipient organizations, and its best motives may be grossly misinterpreted. Yet, in justice to its own citizens and taxpayers it must ask if it is justified in exacting certain conditions when it extends aid and whether it can escape responsibility for the social results of its technical assistance. It must, for example, face the problem of the extent to which self-determinism can be justified in a modern world with shrinking space, dwindling natural resources, and inevitable interaction and influence between nations.

Policy Problems: Control of Material Resources

If it is conceded that foreign agencies are more than merely neutral sources of technical information, then the moral judgements which they will be called upon to make will inevitably touch upon the control of material and of human resources. These are problems which have never proved easy even within national areas. In international relations, where there are widely different cultural backgrounds, they are enormously more difficult, yet cannot be ignored. With regard to the control of material resources, two questions of policy are faced: Who *owns* the natural resources of an under-developed area? and Who *owns* the patent of process right indispensable to the utilization of those natural resources?

It has generally been accepted in the past that a nation owns all rights above and below the soil within its territorial limits. This is equivalent to saying that the accidental owner of surface land owns the undeveloped natural resources within it. Yet the majority of under-developed nations, while claiming the international principle, have rejected it with regard to regions or individuals within their state: in England, for instance, any oil found beneath the surface belongs to the state, not to the owner of the land. Thus, in the community of nations, states claim rights which they refuse to their own citizens. There is yet a further problem: if such indispensable natural resources as subsoil minerals, water, timber, and watersheds, fertility of the soil, fishing and sealing rights are held by the government or by private individuals in an under-developed area, the question arises as to whether they also have the right to control the exploitation of these rights. To be very specific, can they refuse to let the resources be developed? Can they determine who shall use them? And can they determine for what the resources shall be used – for atomic bombs or power for peaceful purposes, for their own luxury or their children's survival? It is commonly held that 'the people' of an area have a moral claim to its riches, but it may be asked what are the limits of this claim and from where does it come? Can a nomadic people, for instance, insist upon continuing its way of life at the cost of harming the rest of the world which needs the resources stored beneath the soil over which it wanders?

One of the most troublesome aspects of this problem is the application of such principles to economic regions which extend beyond politically determined national boundaries. Do the people who are economically dependent upon the resources beyond their national boundaries have a moral, and legal, right to determine the policies for exploiting those resources? Thus, for example, do the people dwelling in the lower basin of a great river have a moral claim to the upper watershed on which their economic survival depends; do the fishermen of one nation have a claim on the schools of fish that pass through coastal waters of another nation; or the steel workers of a coal-poor nation upon the coalfields of their neighbour?

Most of these questions have been at least crudely answered in international law. But a technical-assistance programme which goes no further than the bare legal decision in establishing its policy may be unwittingly storing up political tensions and economic difficulties which ultimately will quite erase its value. When it is a simple case of increasing the yield of a peasant's field by the adoption of better fertilizers, there is little likelihood of difficulty. But when it is a question of discovering, producing, processing, and distributing some subsoil mineral wealth, then the question can be truly grave. What is the relative value of a raw material and an indispensable technical process? Does the undiscovered oil pool lying 8,000 feet below a desert constitute 'real wealth'? Is the technical-assistance policy to be one of giving hybrid seeds to peasants or is it to be that of giving patents and capital for the construction of a plastics factory which will utilize agricultural products to their maximum?

Policy Problems: Control of Human Resources

It is obvious that the utilization of human resources is probably the most important of the moral issues in which technical-assistance policy is involved. It touches upon every aspect of any programme. Who is to benefit? Who shall work and under what conditions? What will be the result of the technical-assistance project on the patterns of population?

The ultimate consequence of assistance is to alter basically social conditions. This may involve incorporating womanpower into productive employment. It may delay the marriage age. It may settle nomadic populations and urbanize rural ones. It may introduce health measures and increase life expectancy while decreasing infantile mortality. It may encourage intensive land utilization and make large families profitable, or it may encourage industrialization and make large families expensive. One set of measures it introduces may be working in opposition to another set. If the foreign donor agency is to be realistic it must face the question of its moral right to tamper with demographic patterns. Does it have the right to supply birth-control techniques in a non-Christian Oriental nation which requests them: yet not have the right to supply the same techniques under similar circumstances in a Roman Catholic nation which opposes them? Should it introduce programmes that it knows will rapidly increase the population of an under-developed area beyond the power of that area to support it, without simultaneously insisting upon economic changes which will correct the trend?

Conditions of Success

Whilst these general questions of policy should be asked, answers which apply to all programmes of development cannot be given. The circumstances of each, though showing similar features, differ considerably in detail. So often factors suggesting the possibility of successful economic and social development are opposed by equally powerful ones militating against it. Thus, whilst one of the objects of analysis is not only to ask the pertinent questions but to state as precisely as possible the conditions for the success of the process, no claim can be made that the contents of the 1954 *Year Book* provide a formula for success.

Yet some attempt might be made to indicate the conditions under which successful programmes have taken and are taking place. That the development of one aspect of a country's economy can produce results is abundantly clear from a study of Aramco's educational programme. Here the conditions are unique. The very reality of immense economic rewards through the winning of oil apparently makes the other factors of minor importance. For with vast underground wealth, relatively easily obtained when advanced Western oil technology is used, the possibility of raising the general standards of living, accumulating capital for further social and educational development is clear. So many of the economic problems of development can be solved and the questions we have asked be answered. The area of development is obvious; what other could indeed be suggested or chosen? The donor providing the technical skill in a country unable to provide it, is in a position to dictate actual technological development plans, whilst, at the same time cautiously avoiding direct participation in the general educational development of the country. The returns from immediate development are so rapid and prodigious that a choice between this and long-range social advancement hardly presents itself. The one so easily follows the former. The questions of organization, whilst presenting problems of detail, are answered in general terms without difficulty. The expertise must be supplied by the assisting country. Almost equally inevitably large numbers of semi-skilled and unskilled workers have to be found locally. The problem resolves itself into one of finding methods of training these skilled and semi-skilled local workers.

Many other questions of policy here find a ready answer. Yet the economic factor should not be regarded as of overriding importance. Examples can be quoted of countries equally rich in natural resources whose programme of economic development has bogged down through political considerations. Thus it is of value to note the social conditions in Saudi Arabia which make this development possible. Here, in a new nation, live a handful of nomadic tribes held together by a common religious culture and an all-powerful – if enlightened –

monarchy. Lay education is not widespread, nationalism in the sense of resistance to outside assistance is not well developed. Yet the general culture, springing from the same Middle-Eastern background as that of the West, is not antagonistic to technical development. The test perhaps will come when national prosperity has brought wider contacts with the West to more of the local population; if and when the flame of nationalism has been fanned and when the inhabitants – perhaps hardly recognizing the great benefits that Western technical aid has bestowed – feel jealous of the economic rewards enjoyed by foreigners for that aid. For under these conditions greater value is placed on the raw materials than on the indispensable technical knowledge required for their development.

Other examples of how development under all-powerful governments can proceed could be given. Where governments, despite popular protest, have been determined to push through programmes of development in selected areas, economic and material improvements have followed but the social consequences have sometimes been disastrous. In their searching for incentives to maintain the morale and sustain the efforts of their people under conditions of hardship and deprivation, the Japanese leaders found nationalism and militarism. The task of democratic governments, sensitive to popular demand, anxious not to place on their people the deprivation often necessary in an economy lacking immediately realizable resources, is more difficult. The pressure in India to spread development programmes horizontally rather than to concentrate the efforts in selected areas is clear. Importance is placed also on winning general support for the programme. If education can play a direct and useful part in the process being carried through by democratic governments it is to make clear that the well-being generally demanded can be achieved only through increased endeavour, greater production, longer hours of work for, in many cases, the same financial rewards.

Resistance to this kind of education is found where suspicion of the motives of the country providing aid is already aroused. In Syria the decision to proceed without foreign assistance, despite the obvious retardation of the process, serves to illustrate the point. The anxiety of the British Development Corporation to make clear its proposal to 'sell-out' some of its projects to local peoples clearly indicates that one of the necessary conditions for successful development is the firm belief of the peoples of the developing country that the fruits of development will be theirs.

If the economic and political conditions favourable for development are reasonably obvious, no criteria – in the form of answers to the policy problems we have stated – in the ethical-social fields are so apparent. In many cases resistance factors to technological development in terms of social patterns emerge. In the 1954 *Year Book* Miss Camilla Wedgewood's account, 'Papua and the Trust Territory of New Guinea', describes conditions so difficult to reconcile with a new technological society that the future adaptation – despite the efforts of the Administration and voluntary agencies – of the natives 'as individuals and as communities to their new environment' is uncertain. Here indeed, many of the economic, political, and social factors come together – in marked contrast to Saudi Arabia – to resist technological development.

The ethical conditions for success are equally difficult to define. Analyses of the possible solutions have been made by Western, Near-Eastern, and Indian philosophers. The diversity of their outlooks – as well as their points of agreement – reveal the fundamental difficulty of answering the problem in general terms.

In these two fields particularly, education as a process of enabling cultural transmission and cultural change to take place harmoniously is of immense importance. Educators of both the receiving and donating countries should study carefully the unique problems associated with this dual task. What is to be retained, what is to be modified, and what of an alien culture can be added without meeting violent opposition so that the whole process of development is not brought to naught by prejudice, suspicion, bad faith, or righteous indignation?

These considerations seem relevant in educational planning; not with the object of finding a panacea but as an attempt to make clear the questions which might be asked and to draw attention to some of the answers, however qualified they might have to be.

The Planning of Cultural Change

It is a feature of the twentieth-century revolution that questions like the above have to be considered at the international level. After all, the Industrial Revolution in North-West Europe and North America was planned by no one. It was the work of individuals seeking their own profit. The concomitant social changes were not foreseen – they happened accidentally. When difficulties occurred, such as extreme poverty or the exploitation of child labour, new institutions were set up to deal with them. But the on-going industrial revolutions in Asia, Africa, and Eastern Europe are very largely initiated, directed, and nourished by governments or other large agencies. Experience has taught us what results may follow, and measures are often taken in advance to minimize harmful effects. In spite of this, industrialization is certain to bring evils in its train, and the more rapid the process the worse these will be. The successes in the Soviet Union were achieved by a ruthless planning and a disregard of individual rights.

In the last two hundred years, the whole world has come to realize what sort of contribution schools can make to economic and social change. When Peter the Great decided to develop shipbuilding and sea-borne trade in Russia he thought it sufficient to take back with him from England a few schoolmasters and craftsmen. When the rulers of the Ottoman Empire in the first half of the nineteenth century decided to build up a modern army, they concluded that a few military colleges would be enough. However, when, in 1870, the group that had obtained power in Japan decided to modernize their Empire they realized that bigger and more complex measures than these would be necessary. They realized that a process of cultural transformation involves careful planning of cultural transmission. State-directed economic revolutions need almost total planning of entire educational systems.

For, as we have insisted more than once in this essay, the process of industrialization means much more than the learning of simple skills. Industrial mass production, as practised in the West, is the outcome of the functioning of a particular kind of society. The skills needed are not merely skills of hand nor even of brain; they are also social. They are habits which are supported by attitudes, traditions, and modes of feeling. What is involved in all this can be gathered from the researches of anthropologists. A rather extreme example is to be found in a book by Jack McLaren, an Australian writer whose wit often disguises, while it adorns, acute observation and wisdom. He describes his attempt to start a plantation on Cape York Peninsula.[1]

[1] Jack McLaren, *My Crowded Solitude* (London: Quality Press Ltd, 1946).

Of course, the natives here are among the most primitive and backward human beings on earth: there is no resemblance between Northern Australia and the countries considered in this essay. Nevertheless, certain points of general significance are brought out in McLaren's story. He selected as his helpers some strong and seemingly intelligent men and persuaded them to set to work.

And now I encountered my first real difficulty, a difficulty indeed which in all the years I was there I never wholly succeeded in overcoming. It was that of teaching the natives the use of European tools. As people accustomed to the implements of the Stone Age in which they lived, implements such as a saw, chisel, hammer, and auger were completely beyond them. Though they were quick to grasp the purposes of these tools, they were exceedingly slow to learn to use them effectively and without damage. Even the most intelligent was liable to buckle a saw within two minutes, the repairing of which would cost me, maybe, a full two hours' work. In fact half my time was occupied in repairing damage caused by my well-intentioned Palaeolithic carpenters.

And so McLaren goes on describing his troubles. The natives would not rise in the morning: they preferred to sit about till late at night gossiping and dancing. The cultural pattern forbade anyone to waken up a sleeper – for when a man slept, his spirit left his body and it would be excessively bad for him to wake without it. They took an infinite time over their meals. They very quickly got tired. They left their jobs on the slightest pretext. If left unsupervised for even a few minutes, they went to sleep. In a word, their total output was very small not merely because of the difficulty they found in handling tools or equipment, but because all their attitudes and behaviours were attuned to a mode of life utterly different from that of an industrialized people. They had not learned the disciplines and habits, the self-control, the time-consciousness, the drives which our own babies pick up from their parents or our youngsters learn in the primary schools. And who was to teach them? In fact, is it really possible to change a cultural pattern according to a pre-established plan?

Certainly, decisions can be made to assist a certain process of transmission, to adopt a particular innovation or to reject another. The trouble is that unexpected social by-products inevitably disturb expectations – a sad fact familiar to reformers everywhere. Nevertheless, faith remains. Societies are modifiable and perfectable. To some degree, man can control his destiny. When he is presented with alternatives he can determine which is better. We believe, too, that an intensive study of a cultural pattern makes it possible to set up desirable goals and to select appropriate means for their realization. We believe that all education involves making value judgements and it is thus moral in nature. We believe that economic issues inevitably influence educational choices, but also that the psychological and anthropological patterns of a society limit and determine these choices.

What is needed is a perception, on the part of those who shape educational policy, of the very great complexity of their task; a realization of the fact that their actions will and should affect every aspect of life. A few examples of this fact, like TVA or the Zuider-Zee project, can be taken from advanced economies to show that even there problems arise which, at their own level, are of one piece with modernization.

If foreign agencies are assisting in the process of transformation, they too have to take account of the side-effects of their actions. An overseas training programme, for example, can return thousands of university graduates to an under-developed nation, yet can utterly fail to solve its needs if they have been selected from parts of the population which are antagonistic to the predicted social change, or if they have received training which does not meet a need in their emerging economy, or if their contact with the foreign culture disturbs and unsettles them for return to their own society. And an industrial training programme which concentrates upon specific techniques may provide the personnel for markedly increased production, but it will make the total technical-assistance programme fail if it regiments the workers and stifles leadership.

Educational Statesmanship

A philosophic perception of the more remote consequences of educational action together with a judicious weighing of alternatives are the marks of statesmanship. Popular clamour and pressure from self-interested petty politicians may often lead to policies which, while attractive at first sight, will fail in the long run. And it is precisely here that leadership must come in, so that the people may see where their true advantage lies.

In the first place, it is essential that the policy makers should be clear regarding aims. For example: if Indians decide that Mahatma Gandhi's ideals of the development of rich community life in the villages and the fostering of local hand-industries are right, the pattern of their educational system will be different from what it would be if the aim were the rapid adoption of modern technology. There is a danger, too, in being over-ambitious. It is probably un-realistic to expect that Indians or Chinese will attain in the next twenty or even fifty years the degree of material prosperity enjoyed by Americans, but quite possible that they will by then catch up, say, with the agricultural nations of Europe. Again, human resources are scarce everywhere, but especially so in under-developed countries. The number of well-educated men and women is small: should this limited supply be directed towards teaching, towards medicine, or towards industrial and agricultural production? If this last fails to grow, the first will lack proper support. But again, unless educational facilities are provided, how can industry prosper? Actually, far too little is known regarding the relation between economic and educational planning[2] – there is here a fruitful field for research. We think with something almost akin to horror of the casual way in which great educational plans, affecting whole countries, are framed. Usually less attention to detail and fact go into them than, say, into the building of a small warship or into the equipping of a minor factory. And nearly always prejudice and blind tradition drive out reason, research, and realization. Here less wishful thinking and more thinkful wishing is needed.

The difficulties of wise policy-making are aggravated by the two great but often distorted passions of the modern world: democracy and nationalism. Without both, nations would have gained neither freedom nor unity. But the price paid is often stultifying.

Egalitarian democratic feeling often expresses itself by a clamant demand for the immediate establishment of universal compulsory education and for the abolition of all privilege. In practice, this means easy access for all to secondary and higher education. Now there is no

[2] For a detailed treatment of this subject see the pp. 73–117 of this volume, and *World Year Book of Education, 1967*: 'Educational Planning'.

doubt that such provisions are wise and economically rewarding, if the resources in teaching personnel and buildings can be provided. It might be profitable to irrigate a desert, making the whole of it fruitful. But if there is available only a little water, which is best: to irrigate only a few acres or to spread it over the entire thirsty area? Europe was fortunate. It built up its educational capital slowly over the centuries, restricting the small amounts available to privileged classes. And this was accepted by the masses who saw the will of God expressing itself by this inequality. But when the time came for quick growth, there were in existence colleges and schools which were capable of training the great numbers of teachers necessary to staff new institutions. This was true of Russia, too, and it may be true of India and the Middle East. In many under-developed countries, however, it is not, and there exists a real danger of a great disappointment in the years to come. Very often the populations of these countries cannot exist at all without the economic contribution made by child labour. How, for instance, are small children best employed in countries like China? Should they gather sticks for fuel and help to cultivate the fields? Would it really be better for them to learn reading and writing while going cold and hungry? Wise policy making will express itself here by the laying of plans of educational development which apportion resources rightly between the various levels of education, paying attention to the paramount need for selection, training of leaders and of professional *élites*. It will express itself, too, by the degree to which it endeavours to consolidate progress and change achieved, by plans for the provision of public libraries, museums, and all other agencies of adult education.

The difficulties that come from exacerbated national feeling are even more puzzling than those created by misdirected democratic ideals. Language problems are a good example. For instance, from the economic point of view India stands to gain from a widespread knowledge of English, which is helpful in commerce and which is the key to a very rich technical and scientific literature. Yet the standards of teaching this language are falling rapidly and its importance in the schools is diminishing. Worse still: many areas of India are now beginning to ask that their own regional language take precedence over the federal language, Hindustani or Hindi. Success here might actually hamper the growth of prosperity. And what of the attempts made in many countries to foster the learning of languages which were dying out? Is it always wise to invent alphabets and to provide literatures in primitive languages? Are we certain that the adoption of this policy in some regions of the earth was the result only of an unselfish desire to foster culture and not at all to the application of a divide-and-rule policy? Sir Olaf Caroe,[3] in a book dealing with Central Asia, has interesting things to say on this point.

Again, it is obvious to all that developments in the newly independent nations of Asia would be facilitated if more Western aid and supervision in education were provided. But national feeling will not allow it: such help has to be carefully controlled and hedged about. In many countries even immigration is now looked upon with disfavour. Yet it continues to be of importance. For instance, the contributions made by the Jewish refugees from Hitler's tyranny greatly benefited Turkey and South America. Israel itself is a nation which is at the moment possibly the most erudite in the world and which has an unprecedented concentration of skill. Far from being poor, this young nation has an investment in training so great that it cannot profitably exploit it to the full.

Cultural Change and Education

What has been said makes it clear that what is needed is the creation of a theory of education more complex and relevant than anything available. Our hope is that the 1954 *Year Book* made an acceptable contribution towards the formulation of this theory, in presenting special papers by expert contributors illustrated and expanded by case studies dealing with specially significant areas and problems. Where opinions were sharply divided, contributions from both sides of the controversy were sought. The section on aims, objectives and implications of technological development was, we believe, of pre-eminent importance. As has been argued above, it is not in the details of production techniques and educational methods that technical-assistance or community-development plans fail, but in the establishment of their fundamental philosophy. In establishing a theory it is necessary to examine the laws of social change and the

---

[3] *Wells of Power: The Oilfields of South-Western Asia* (London: Macmillan, 1951).

problems of the social setting in which development programmes operate. This expresses our belief that anthropology and sociology are the ancillary sciences which, above all, have a contribution to make to the new theory of education we look for. We think, too, that at each of the levels of development, education and schooling have a vital part to play. Instrumentally, schools can do much to induce nomadic tribes to settle in one spot, they can help to bring remote tribes into contact with a richer and more advanced culture, they can provide useful knowledge to peasants and help them to meet their needs. And culturally, too, education can do much to stabilize the emotional and social life of human beings who are disoriented through the breaking up of habitual patterns and who are more or less lost in a strange new world. It should be noted, incidentally that examples can be drawn from very backward areas as well as from advanced industrialized countries. For the whole world, in truth, is experiencing the impact of the on-going economic, social, and cultural revolution. We are all, to some degree, men of two cultures immersed in the past and yet facing the atomic age. The history of Japan since the Meiji restoration is fascinating, for example, because it is the story of an important and successful case of cultural transmission.

Little more need be said, except that in all cases of cultural and economic transformation, the impact of Western culture should be critically examined. Similarly the problem of social evaluation of the results of technical assistance should also be considered. The reporting of results achieved by a given programme has unfortunately frequently been both inadequate and doctrinaire. A public-health team has reduced the mortality at childbirth or greatly lowered the incidence of malaria in some relatively unimportant village or isolated mountain valley. An anti-illiteracy team has taught a certain percentage of the adults of some tribe or area to read. Often the importance of these achievements has been grossly inflated. Sometimes the implications for the final goal of technical assistance have been badly misinterpreted. The cost of such a programme must be considered: for with unlimited capital almost any result may be achieved. Green vegetables, for example, can be grown on the sterile surface of a concrete slab. Yet unless the process becomes self-supporting it will ultimately depress, rather than raise, the material standard of living –

or alternatively demand continued assistance from some paternalistic outside source. But even if the programme can be financed, can be expanded to a large-scale endeavour – and can produce the immediate results claimed – this does not necessarily constitute an unqualified success. An adequate evaluation must measure the impact upon social and political life, and their relation to simple indices of economics, health, and education. But the final evaluation can come only from those persons whose burden has been lightened and whose society has been altered. How well has the programme achieved their dream of a better life?

BIBLIOGRAPHY

Cerych, Ladislav. *Problems of Aid to Education in Developing Countries.* (Praeger Special Studies in International Economics and Development) New York/London, Praeger, for the Atlantic Institute, 1965.
'The aim of the present study is to define the essential features of a consistent policy of external aid to education, the conditions for making it more effective and the means by which it can be extended and co-ordinated internationally.'

Coleman, James S. (editor). *Education and Political Development.* Princeton, University Press, 1965. xii, 620 pp.
The problem analysed in this volume is what part education plays in

the process of modernization, and what the real relationships are between political policies and educational processes. Developing and developed systems are both represented in more than fourteen case-studies.

Etzioni, Amitai and Eva. *Social Change: Sources, Patterns, and Consequences.* New York/London, Basic Books 1964. xii, 503 pp. This comprehensive reader includes a representative selection of 50 'classic' and contemporary writings on social change. Problems covered include: innovation, modernization, theories of history, roles of institutions.

Hauser, Philip M. and Schnore, Leo F. *The Study of Urbanization.* New York/London, Wiley, 1965. This is a comprehensive account of research in urbanization presenting an inventory and appraisal of the study of urbanization in such fields as economics, geography, history, political science, sociology and anthropology.

Horowitz, Irving Louis. *Three Worlds of Development: The Theory and Practice of International Stratification.* New York, Oxford University Press 1966. xiv, 475 pp. The U.S.A. and her Western allies, the U.S.S.R. and the Eastern Bloc, and the 'Third World' of Asia, Africa and Latin America are considered in terms of social, political, economic, military and psychological development.

Japanese National Commission for Unesco (editor). *The Role of Education in the Social and Economic Development of Japan.* (Tokyo), Ministry of Education, 1966. ix, 429 pp. This is an extensive analysis of the role education played in the social and economic development of Japan since the Meiji Restoration in 1868. Conclusions on the role of education in social and economic development can be applied to developing countries, especially in Asia and Africa.

Lave, Lester B. *Technological Change: Its Conception and Measurement.* Englewood Cliffs, Prentice Hall, 1966. xx, 228 pp. This is an attempt at defining technological change. Not only is the literature reviewed, but the author tries to synthesize various theories and methods. The educational background and implications are well covered.

Mead, Margaret (editor). *Cultural Patterns and Technical Change*. (Tensions and Technology) Paris, Unesco 1953, reprint 1956. 348 pp.

The Unesco resolutions which brought this work about were: 'to study possible methods of relieving tension caused by the introduction of modern techniques in non-industrialized countries and those in process of industrialization'; and 'to bring together and diffuse existing knowledge and to encourage studies of the methods of harmonizing the introduction of modern technology in countries in process of industrializations, with respect for their cultural values so as to ensure the social progress of the peoples.'

Redfield, Robert. *Human Nature and the Study of Society*: (The papers of Robert Redfield, Volume I). Edited by Margaret Park Redfield. Chicago/London, Chicago University Press, 1962. xvi, 507 pp.

The first part of the book deals with general theory of anthropology; the second part contains a discussion of Redfield's work in Mexico and papers on primitive society and the nature of civilization; the final section deals with the question of 'whether there is a common "nature" shared by all human beings and on the way in which cultures interrelate'.

Redfield, Robert. *The Little Community-and-Peasant Society and Culture*. Chicago/London, Chicago University Press 1965. v, 182, 92 pp.

The first essay is an exploration into the means by which human communities can be understood. The second essay shows how the study of anthropology can transfer from the study of primitive society to complex civilized societies.

Spindler, George E. *Education and Culture – Anthropological Approaches*. New York/London, Holt, Rinehart and Winston, 1963. xx, 571 pp.

This book explores the application of anthropology to education:

how culture is transmitted and how values are activated by education passed on. A special section deals with the problem in American culture and another presents a cross-cultural view.

Zollschan, George K. and Hirsch, Walter (editors). *Explorations in Social Change*. London, Routledge, 1964. xxviii, 832 pp.

In this volume social change is studied from sociological, anthropological, historical, economical, philosophical and political points of view. Conclusions for future development are made by social planners.

Education and Economics

from the 1956 Year Book of Education
Robert King Hall
Joseph A. Lauwerys

In the south-east corner of Iran, close to the frontiers of Pakistan and Afghanistan, there is a nomadic tribe which ranges over an area about the size of France. This tribe, the Baluchi, are best known to the few tourists who visit them for the beautiful rugs they weave and the enormously impressive moustaches which their men affect. They are an ancient people, proud and highly effective in their nomadism, although almost completely illiterate. They are, indeed, almost the prototype of a technologically under-developed society, and their economic level is amongst the lowest in the world. It has been shown that the Baluchi are incapable of providing even a minimum of formal education for their children, in spite of any possible utilization of their present economy. Even if they did not spend a single penny on food, clothing, or shelter, and if they saved nothing for future security or defence, they would still not create enough wealth to cover the exceedingly modest cost of the elementary education made compulsory by Iranian law.

A situation like this raises a basic question: How much education can a society afford? To which Americans would probably reply that the real question was rather whether any society could 'afford' to do without education. This is correct for rich and complex societies, where a literate and highly trained population is needed, but misleading when applied to impoverished or relatively primitive ones. In the U.S.A., education is recognized and rewarded materially and spiritually. There is a widespread belief that man has it in his power to modify his situation and to improve his lot through his own efforts.

This faith is rooted in the deep-seated optimism of a young, dynamic, and growing society in which there is little fear of defeat or failure. It is sustained by a national economy capable of providing almost any level of material well-being, provided the apparatus at hand is used intelligently, forcefully and skilfully. Education, then, appears as a social instrument through which man can guide his destiny and shape his future.

Human societies do not all enjoy the wealth and natural resource of the U.S.A., nor share the energy and optimism of Americans. Often, there is fear of the future and love of the past; the will to seek modest security rather than dangerous greatness. The essential point for the philosopher to note is that everywhere ideas on the upbringing of the young stem from and reflect historical experiences, geographical conditions, and patterns of culture.

It is a truism that all societies have an adequate educational system, for if they did not they would vanish. All cultures teach a language which, however primitive in form or restricted in vocabulary, is adequate for immediate needs. All transmit the essential secrets of sex and reproduction, as well as the knowledge needed to survive. The Baluchi, for example, teach their young an array of difficult and complex skills by which they secure the minimum necessary requirements in one of the most cruelly arid regions of the globe. It is difficult to know just what advice could be given to them by even the most skilled Western consultants, unless new sources of wealth were discovered.

It seems that our question might well be re-stated as:What is the level of education which is desirable for a given group? The answer would be that this level is determined in part by the economic capacity of the group, in part by the skills required for survival, in part by the values accepted. The ability to find water and to maintain direction in a desert waste have high priority with a nomadic tribe. They have no importance in the city of New York. The American youngster is given intensive instruction in safety rules and traffic problems, while attention is paid to the vocational choices which he will have to make in a highly industrialized environment. The Baluchi do not need to read or write, but do need to understand the psychology of camels. The young American can hardly recognize a camel when he sees one in the Bronx Zoo, but may well have the movements of his eyeballs analysed to improve his speed of reading. And he will study the psychology of group processes while learning the complicated human relations which occur in industrialized societies based upon scientific technology.

These are extremes. But similar, though smaller, differences are noted between cultures which are superficially alike. Only a narrow channel separates Britain from France, only a political frontier lies between Germany and Belgium. Yet there are marked differences between the educational practices these nations pursue. Take another example: both the U.S.A. and the U.S.S.R. are dedicated to the education of the masses. In some ways, the outer structures of their school systems resemble each other. Yet how different are the results! It is the social and political philosophy adopted which shapes the aims: as is society, so is education.

In order to clarify the point, let us consider another simple case or model. The *guru* of ancient India served his community as an educator. Through him the lore of the *Vedas* was passed on. He was the agent through whom learning was disseminated; social norms perpetuated; religious, political, and medical knowledge imparted; the arts of war preserved. His task required lengthy training and the utmost devotion. In time, it became the privilege and responsibility of the Brahmins. Each teacher had a small number of pupils, who lived with him. Those who could not pay for the education they received were expected to gather fuel, collect food by begging, and do household chores for the *guru*. Students often lived for as many as twelve years with their teacher and, understandably, the number living in the household at any time was restricted to fewer than two dozen. Education was thus provided in the powerful institution of the household and family. For his support the *guru* fulfilled certain important social tasks. He officiated at ceremonies and was responsible for religious ministrations. His class, the sacerdotal, was the first to acquire the rigidity of caste and to become impregnated with various taboos which helped to maintain its sanctity.

In the light of events, it can be seen that the education thus provided made for a stable society, slow to change and regulated by the esoteric knowledge of a minority, for the literature which was its special concern included instructions and information on every aspect of social life. The auxiliary sciences were both theoretical and practical. The system strengthened existing institutions, particularly the family, and was supported by them. The material needs of the teacher were met through the family, he was freed from other duties in order to devote himself to study and teaching, and he either remained within the precincts of a particular house or travelled from one household to another. Begging and patronage were regarded as justifiable methods of acquiring support. The Brahmin lived simply without ostentation, but enjoyed the highest prestige as a result of the duties he performed. Evidently what was, and continued to be, a service to the community became a vested interest and remained so in India until very recently. Under these circumstances education was turned into the privilege of a few and enabled these to maintain their position, sometimes to the disadvantage of the rest of society. For the traditional forms of education may be in conflict with the aspirations of large groups of the people, especially in periods of change. This, however, is another point to which we shall return.

The Economic Aspects of Education

For the present, let us content ourselves by noting that the amount as well as the kind of education demanded is related to the totality of social forms, to the cultural pattern as a whole. One aspect of that pattern is, of course, the economic: the way in which material goods are produced, distributed, and exchanged. There are relationships between the educational and the economic aspects of the total pattern. What we have said should make clear that we do not think this exhausts the discussion. It is obvious that every human activity has its economic aspect, but we reject the view that the latter is essential or fundamental or primary. Undoubtedly, all education has economic aims and its form and content are affected by the economic capacity of the community being served. But that is not the whole story, nor even, perhaps, its most significant or interesting chapter.

In order to study the relations between education and economics, it is helpful to think for a while of the former as if it were a commodity like any other, such as, for example, music or – shall we say? – soap, and then to ask what sorts of question would arise if such goods were being considered. First, of course, would come the problem of demand. What makes a population desire music or soap? What influences bring about an increase or a diminution in demand? Can it be stimulated or diminished? Then, secondly, to produce goods like music or soap resources have to be provided: manpower, materials likely to be scarce, buildings, and so on. How are these resources acquired and allocated? Is the matter left only to the initiative of private persons? Is there any interference by the authorities – as might happen negatively with harmful drugs or positively with religious buildings? Thirdly, what problems of management arise? How are the workers trained? What fixes their remuneration? Fourthly, what determines the price of the product? Are there varying qualities of it, for which varying prices will be paid? Are there subsidies? Fifthly, what economic consequences flow as a result of producing just these goods? A distinction is often drawn here between producer goods, the supply of which increases the capital resources of a community (that is, its capacity to produce what it desires), and consumer goods, which disappear when used. Is education to be classed among producer goods or among consumer goods? Or are there various kinds of 'education', some of which belong to one class while the rest belong to the other?

These are some of the questions which came to our minds when we decided to study the intricate problem we had set ourselves – that of the relation of education to economics. The approach was evidently fruitful and stimulating. But, unfortunately, we soon discovered a quite appalling shortage of factual inquiries. It appeared that far too little work had been done to make it possible for us to realize our plan with complete success. The studies and papers published in the 1956 *Year Book* were, in many cases, little more than tentative explorations of almost virgin land. There is here an almost unlimited field for educational research of high significance at this period of rapid technological change; research which would provide a solid base for the planning of the educational statesman.

The Demand for Education

Let us begin, then, by considering the forces and influences which create a demand for education. Among the Baluchi, evidently, it is as weak as the demand for soap! But in ancient India, the religious and philosophical outlook of the population led them to attach value to what the *guru* taught. The Indians met problems in their daily life and perplexities within their minds which, as they saw, could be solved or simplified if the counsel or instruction of the teacher were accepted. In general, indeed, the religious sentiment has everywhere and always led to the stimulation of demand for instruction of a particular kind: in the right rituals and ceremonials, in the skills needed to read the sacred texts, in the philosophical interpretation of the sayings and epigrams of the holy men. It is here, too, that the activities of missionaries belong, whether Christian, Muslim, or Buddhist. They, too, by spreading religious faith, helped to stimulate demand for a particular kind of education.

At first, religious teachers are always maintained willingly by gifts of food or hospitality or alms. But already this support involves a diversion of material resources: only seldom, as in the medieval monasteries of Christendom, do wise and holy men actually till the soil or engage in the manipulation of materials. Usually they produce goods that are desired, as are music and art. By so doing they help to maintain individual and social harmony, cohesion and morale. Indirectly, no doubt, this helps the production of fundamental necessities – food, shelter, defence – but only indirectly. At a later stage, these same religious men may also teach crafts and usable skills: as did the monks who introduced the plough and a knowledge of the working of metals to the barbarians of the North. Here they intervened directly, and contributed to economic well-being. Perhaps, however, this should be considered rather as an instance of intercultural contact than as an example of the effect of the religious sentiment. And quite certainly, one of the permanently powerful agencies stimulating the demand for education is precisely the external stimulus due to such contacts. A vigorous and expanding people – the Romans in the Ancient World or the British in the eighteenth or nineteenth centuries – extends its dominion and its trading area. The indigenous population with which it has relations – the Gauls or the Indians – desires to possess the knowledge which brings power. The conquerors, on the other hand, need the services of clerks, administrators, and soldiers. They allot resources for education and training. The demand exists, the supply is created.

And sometimes the whole society, while retaining political independence and even autonomy, changes within itself in the effort to acquire what is possessed by those who are richer or more advanced. The rulers of the less developed society may set themselves both to create demand and to organize supply – as happened in Russia a generation ago and is happening in China now. Here a new factor nearly always comes in. The rulers desire not education in general, but education of a particular kind; aimed at industrial advance and at political docility. They look for a selective valve. There can be little doubt that the complex *Kanamajiri* system of writing in Japan was deliberately used as such a valve through which was transmitted only the knowledge which the ruling groups desired the people to have. The entire structure of the Japanese State, developed under the theory of the *Kokutai*, depended upon the proper functioning of this valve. There is just as little doubt that the enormous and expensive educational system of Soviet Russia has for thirty-five years been used not only to transmit vocational skills but also to control political and social beliefs. Even in countries which pride themselves on offering great freedom of dissent to individuals, in the United States, Great Britain, Sweden, Switzerland, or Chile, for instance, one finds that the population is surprisingly susceptible to the manipulation of thoughts, beliefs, attitudes, and emotions by the very educational apparatus which is believed to be the instrument and guarantee of freedom.

As social change proceeds, the nature of the demand for education changes too. What satisfied at an earlier time no longer does. In medieval Europe, schools and colleges were built by the direct labour of monks or by the money provided by wealthy bishoprics. The church dominated the educational process and provided the ideological leadership needed to direct military and social power into acceptable channels. No doubt the prime purpose was the maintenance and expansion of the institution itself, but incidental benefits accrued. When conditions changed through the voyages of discovery, the development of mechanical invention, and the incipient industrial revolution of the seventeenth century, the nature of the demand changed too. Milton asked for an education 'which fits a man to perform justly, skilfully, and magnanimously all the offices both private and public of peace and war', thus expressing his dissatisfaction with the wordy, literary education suited to earlier times. His curriculum extended far beyond grammar – though he starts with that – to the study of applied agriculture and engineering, to household economics, politics, law, and the highest matters of theology. The study of politics was, he thought, desirable for students collected together in groups of about one hundred and fifty in spacious houses set aside for the purpose in 'every city throughout the land'. Through it 'they may not in a dangerous fit of the Commonwealth be such poor, shaken uncertain reeds of such tottering conscience, as many of our great counsellors have lately shown themselves, but steadfast pillars of the State'.

The needs of the time were for men trained in the applied sciences – trigonometry, architecture, engineering, and navigation. Commercial enterprise was creating a demand for trained personnel which could not be provided by the traditional schools and universities. Milton recognized the need. He also wrote as one committed to a defence of parliamentary democracy against a king who based his authority to rule on 'Divine Right'.

Thus in Milton is found an educational pioneer who recognized the needs of commerce and the needs of political democracy. Whilst vested interests have continued to resist the demands of groups interested in these aspects of education, the latter have gradually come to the forefront. To their claims has been added the social demand for technically trained personnel. This is a late-nineteenth- and twentieth-century demand.

Historic examples can be quoted of institutions which owe their birth, or extension, to one or several of these three demands. The rapid growth in nineteenth-century England of the 'Public' school was connected with an increasing demand for educated people who would run England's expanding commercial enterprises. These had involved the annexation, subjection, or simple occupation of many foreign countries for the purposes of trade. An empire needed administrators, and it is due to more than chance that the nineteenth-century English 'Public' schools were able to supply it.

German education stands in the same period as an example of a system responding to various social demands, one of the most significant of which was industrialization, which required technical-vocational training. The efficiency of the German *Fachschule*, *Berufschule*, and *Technische Hochschule* system bears witness to the clarity with which the leaders of German unification and nationalism saw the role of education in the international race for industrial supremacy.

The original intentions of the early European settlers in America to provide education in order to defeat the old deluder Satan were transformed after the Revolution into a clear-cut desire to maintain through an educational system the democratic institutions which the founding fathers cherished and which they thought the best defence against the Satan of personal power and the corruption which it brings.

Allied to all such demands has been yet another, due to the creation of sovereign states. Nationalism itself has been a powerful incentive and stimulus to the provision of education on a wide scale. It has taken many forms, depending upon where national leaders have thought security to lie, but it has always involved a demand for an education that would help to produce good, loyal, patriotic citizens.

Then there are the changes in the class structure of society which come from changes in trade, political organization, and industrial life. Though the Marxian predictions and prophecies of doom are unacceptable to most Western people, yet Marx's analysis of the economic conditions promoting social change has much to commend it. The development of a very large educated middle class capable of industrial management and control has made it possible for some societies to avoid the ultimate and final clash between *bourgeoisie* and proletariat. This development is the result of a combined demand by the leaders for an education that would safeguard democracy and by the masses for educational opportunities that would lead to higher social and economic status and, perhaps incidentally, would help them to participate in the government of their country.

If the Marxian thesis is wrong, it must be possible for those who control the means of production, on the one hand, and for the wage-earners on the other, to recognize their interdependence and so to modify their attitudes and institutions as to lead to mutual satisfaction and confidence. An educational system explicitly accepting the aim of fostering institutions through which these processes take place is marked off from all past systems. It implies that the acquisition of education need not out of sheer necessity lead to the acquisition of the political power and to the domination of one class by another.

The democratic ideal also creates its own demand for education. It is expressed, as are all demands for education, through institutions and through groups of people. Commercialism, industrialization, nationalism, and democracy have contributed in various degrees to make the demand for education in most present-day societies a popular one. Clearly, in countries which have recently become independent, like India, there is ambivalence. Her leaders hope that education can make the country democratic and economically prosperous at one and the same time. What do the masses want? As likely as not, their chief concern is with the economic fundamentals of life. Such popular desires are stirred in the twentieth century by the speed of communication and the presence of mass media like the press, radio, and television.

Acquiring Resources for Education

When there is a strong demand for education or instruction, it is, of course, provided. This means that resources have to be allocated to it: manpower is withdrawn from other activities, special buildings may be erected, books and materials provided. Only very seldom, however, is either the total amount or the kind of education left to the ordinary mechanism of supply and demand, that is, to the desires of individual persons prepared to pay the full cost. It is true that there have long existed private academies or schools which charge their customers fees so high as to cover the real cost and which provide exactly the kind of teaching that is desired by the consumers. But even in the Free Cities of the Middle Ages, the burghers saw that some members of their class or estate needed help, at least at a certain period of their life, and they were prepared to club together to maintain schools which were either free or at least charged amounts much below the real economic cost. As for the church, its spiritual and moral power was such that it was able, and still is, to persuade some people to give their services freely as schoolmasters: the aim being to promote the public good through the support of an institution which guards it. Many a father, sceptical and anti-clerical, has sent his sons to a church school, giving them an education of which he approved only in part because it was provided at much less than cost.

It might indeed be argued that education differs from other economic goods because its price has never anywhere been left simply to the play of market demand. The authorities and the *élite* have always interfered. Both have always wanted to have more education than was available and usually education different in kind from that called for by consumers.

They have expressed their will by placing material resources at the disposal of education – on stated conditions. Thus, in the Middle Ages, kings, bishops, and nobles gave land – the source of material wealth – to endow colleges or schools. Rich men left scholarships for deserving boys in their wills, or endowed Chairs of Philosophy at universities. And even today, in countries as progressive and liberal as the United States, so full of faith in the wisdom of private enterprise, we find that federal aid is provided to correct the market in order to enlarge the supply of technological, commercial, or agricultural instruction. And, everywhere, the central government provides instruction for the armed forces, thus helping to keep down the cost of the specialized services it needs and uses.

In a complete treatise on the relation to economic life, this would be the place to consider and to survey carefully the character of the material resources which the provision of educational facilities requires. We should consider what was and what is demanded in the way of manpower, equipment, buildings. We should take into account how these can be enlisted: it would be necessary to weigh up against one another the efficacy of the ideological or humanitarian appeal to which missionaries respond, and the strength of promising security, holidays, and pensions in recruiting personnel for the schools. We should discuss what sort of resources can be directed towards education: whether land or specialized personnel are properly to be thus made available (e.g., it has recently been suggested that scientists and technologists ought to be ordered to teach. What would be the effect of this? We should take into account the by-products of such action on the general economy). We should think about the sales of services or of goods produced by students, not overlooking Mahatma Gandhi's schemes. We should also pay attention to the sale of services rendered by faculty members – to royalties, patents, consultations, fees – for these are quickly becoming a major source of income, especially to the senior staff of universities who are thus compensated for teaching instead of entering the world of commerce and industry. This would lead us to the contribution made by private industry, by either the provision of courses within their concerns, the payment of special taxes, or the release of employees.

Then would come a study of the effects of the philanthropic impulse manifested today in the activities of the Foundations. It would

be fascinating to trace the history of institutions such as the Rockefeller, Carnegie, Ford, or Nuffield Foundations: the economic effects
of the transfer of funds from industry to education and research, the
implicit conditions associated with the gifts, the final effect of this
allocation of resources.

It goes without saying, however, that the most important questions today arise in connexion with the multifarious operation of the
tax machines controlled by public authorities. Education was one of
the first social services to be subsidized from taxation. Much of the
money made available to it came from the obvious source of wealth
of that time, i.e. land and property. As this form of wealth has become
less and less important there has been a shift in the base of taxation.
In England, the cost of education is shared between taxes raised
locally through rates, and those raised nationally on incomes and
consumer goods. Local taxes are assessed on the supposed value of
real estate. The proportion of money from central funds has continued to rise not only in England and France but in most industrialized countries. This may have come about as a result of the inability
of local taxation systems quickly to follow changes in the source of
'wealth'. It may also account for the generally low investment in
education in periods of inflation. For whilst the selling price of
property may rise sharply, its value for the purposes of taxation may
lag very considerably. Yet the property tax is one which can be
administered locally more easily than it can on a national level. The
willingness of communities to pay high 'rates' or property taxes
reflects their preparedness to support education.

The implications of this are important. The operation of tax systems
needs to be analysed if a better understanding of educational problems
is to be obtained. Some of the relevant questions relate to the willingness of taxpayers to support education as a social service compared
with their willingness to support it as an item of personal consumption.
From this point of view an analysis of the acquisition of resources for
education in England and the distribution of benefits is very significant.

Where the greater part of the money is provided from central
funds, and therefore today from non-property taxes, it seems likely
that a larger proportion of the national revenue will be spent on
education than under conditions where the money is raised locally. A
typical example of this is France, where the percentage is as high as

eight. This reflects the appreciation of the political leaders of the social importance of education.

Rejection of an educational programme by refusal to pay taxes would have to be on a national level. The extent to which French municipalities are shifting the burden of education to the central government illustrates the difficulties experienced in raising money locally. This in turn reflects, perhaps, the lowered value of education in France as a consumer item.

It cannot be assumed that the amount of money raised will be proportionately less where money is raised for education largely on a local tax base. If the type of education provided is of a kind which the public appreciate, i.e., if it is a consumer item, then it is likely that local taxation will bring in more money than central funds. The situation in the United States should be studied in these terms. How far has its flexibility, its ability to modify curricular offerings, its comparative freedom from hard and fast traditional educational norms, made it possible to raise locally such a large proportion of the money needed to finance education? And how far has the system of decentralized control made education more modifiable in terms of consumer demand?

If education is to be regarded as a consumer item it has to be responsive to consumer demand. Decentralized control makes this possible. It is pointless, for example, to deplore the reluctance of municipalities in France to shoulder the burden of education if curriculum, organization, appointment, and dismissal of teachers and so on are centrally controlled. Of course, if education is seen as a social service, central administration has many advantages provided, the institutions operating alongside the schools make it difficult for the latter to be manipulated towards political ends by unscrupulous people. The central government may then be expected to provide most of the funds. It can explain its policy in terms of social usefulness, and respond to suggestions for improving this usefulness. It is worth repeating that many administrations fail to distinguish between a social service and a consumer item. They justify their policy in terms of consumer demand when in fact it is a kind of social service. This justification allows them to administer the service as though it were a consumer item, but with 'experts' deciding what the consumer wants.

The Allocation of Resources

In any modern society, many other public services compete with education for trained personnel, buildings, and equipment. In England the atomic research establishment at Harwell, for example, attracts to its service large numbers of the most highly qualified scientists and technicians who might otherwise teach in schools. The armed forces themselves call for many technically trained men and women. Governmental priorities in the United Kingdom and elsewhere often place at the disposal of these armed forces resources far in excess of what the national economy can easily support. Few deny the need for armaments, but it is doubtful whether the large absorption of personnel is cheerfully accepted by the majority of people.

Other political and vote-catching policies tend to attract resources towards areas where popular demand is strong, for example to housing schemes and other social services. Frequently such resources are distributed as a result of powerful labour pressure. The employment of a very high number of supernumerary workers on the railways and in public transportation is a case in point.

The health service is an example of a policy which enjoys the support of a very wide public. Medical knowledge has advanced very rapidly in recent years. With the aid of new drugs, antibiotics, and improved anaesthetics, the power of the medical profession to prevent and cure illness has raced ahead. Health is thought to be within the grasp of all who can avail themselves of the latest medical knowledge and experience. Since most people would rather be alive than educated, this is a field in which popular demand is extremely strong. In most countries resources are being found, both in cash and in kind, to maintain an efficient medical service. This appears to be so whether under a socialized or national health scheme, as in the United Kingdom, or under a free-enterprise system, as in the United States.

Education, indeed, is at a disadvantage *vis-à-vis* all these public services, and this fact is reflected in the generally low salaries of teachers throughout the world – a situation described in the 1953 *Year Book* on the 'Social Position of Teachers'.[1] More often than not, school buildings are more out of date than others. The criteria of efficient education which can be measured in terms of economic re-

---

[1] See also *Essays in Comparative Education*, 'Teachers and Teaching', in this series.

sources, like teacher-pupil ratios, space per pupil, the quantity and quality of specialized equipment, playgrounds, audio-visual aids, and textbooks, are usually laid down by educators. The provision of these necessary ingredients nearly always falls far below the level regarded as adequate.

This level, incidentally, is rising all the time. A hundred years ago all that was needed for an elementary school was a blackboard, rough furniture, and a few cheap booklets. Cheap microscopes, knives, and porcelain dishes sufficed to equip a medical faculty. Today television sets, movie projectors, gymnasiums, and playing-fields are often provided even for young children, while professors of medicine ask for lavish supplies of expensive chemicals, electron microscopes, and laboratory technicians. And universities find it necessary to invest millions in electronic computing gear and the staff needed to operate it. Just as a modern factory needs expensive modern machinery, so does a modern teaching plant – but the latter is always far behind what would be thought proper for the former. The equipment of schools is usually a generation or two behind the times.

When the total amount of support to be devoted to education has been decided, usually with very little insight into the nature of the pressures that have determined the answer, there remains the vast problem of how to distribute the support within education itself. In a money economy, this problem appears as one of somehow reconciling conflicting financial claims within a limited budget. For example, vocational and technical education compete with general education or with mass-literacy campaigns; higher education with secondary or primary schooling; teachers' salaries with the provision of buildings, textbooks, and apparatus. The policy which determines the wise apportioning of resources is influenced by all kinds of factors and conditions vary from country to country. For example, in France, the rapid development of secondary and technical education might be secured by giving money to the Catholic Church – but this would offend a politically influential section of the people. In the southern regions of the U.S.A. much capital has been invested during the last twenty years in the attempt to improve the educational facilities available to Negroes: this was a response to the claims of liberal social thought as well as to the pressure exerted by the coloured population.

Furthermore, there are always decisions to be made connected with the most effective use of existing resources. Thus – should industry, commercial organizations, government departments, or the armed forces rather than schools and colleges undertake certain kinds of vocational training? Would efficiency be increased if they did? If the state bears the cost of technical colleges, industry is provided with recruits which it would otherwise have to train – is this a disguised subsidy to some industries? Who should benefit from this investment? Evidently, the answers given to such questions in highly industrialized countries may differ very much from those appropriate to agricultural ones undergoing mechanization.

Education and Production

It would be easier to arrive at a wise and acceptable policy for allocating available resources if one really knew how to assess the return on educational investment. Unfortunately, only vague and general estimates can be made. For our present purpose, it must suffice to say that the investment should lead to economic improvement. Now, classical economists list four basic elements which, operating jointly, determine the level of production within a community. These are: capital and capital goods, including tools, plant, cash, and credit; a supply of raw materials which is either controlled by or at least accessible to the producing units; transportation from the source of supply and to the markets; and labour. This last factor, which concerns us particularly, consists of skilled labour in the form of a trained working force and managerial talent with skills in leadership and in industrial judgement.

The factors which limit the development of skilled labour can themselves conveniently be grouped under four categories. The first is the availability of inborn, inherited talent. It might be argued that under special conditions a society could concentrate selected characteristics through selective breeding. This could, of course, take place without conscious direction simply as the result of social or natural factors in the environment. Whether it has occurred in the past or not is a matter for speculation, but it is certain that no modern society, whatever its political or social structure, attempts to modify the quality of its working force by planned breeding of human beings.

The second factor which determines the size of the work force is

(2) the availability of institutionalized instruction and of appropriate cultural tools: schools, teachers, libraries, research, language. The Inca Empire was stopped in its growth and ultimately disappeared because it failed to make the indispensable cultural invention of a writing-system capable of accumulating and transmitting knowledge. The Baluchi have no schools and cannot support 'non-productive members of society' such as teachers. Their language is an inadequate vehicle for advanced and systematic thought.

(3)   The third factor, which we have already discussed, is the availability of support. In many parts of the world, this material base, on which an educational system could be founded, simply does not exist. It still has to be created: and this creation may involve a change in the very nature of the cultural pattern itself. For instance, nomadic tribes wandering over a desert followed by a few camels and fat-tailed sheep will have to settle down in fixed abodes. Many, though not all, pastoral economies will have to change to the more productive small-grain agriculture. For some societies with high population densities, even intensive land utilization like wet-paddy rice culture may prove inadequate, and manufacturing industry may have to be developed.

(4)   A fourth element might be called the 'social climate': unless there exists within a society a pattern of attitudes which accords a higher status to an educated than to an uneducated man, people will not seek education. The 'social climate' should include traditions of personal drive in the effort to secure training and skill, as things which are both necessary and desirable. It should also make it possible to grant to those who succeed in acquiring great learning a prestige as high as that given to those who have gained wealth or power by controlling factories or armies.

The real measure of a society's attitude towards education is the recognition it gives to those who are engaged in it and by its willingness to support non-productive members of a society during the process. It will be measured, too, by the use made of skilled talent once it is trained, and by a generalized willingness to accept changes in the cultural mores when these are dictated by the research and experience of educated *élites*. It may well be argued, indeed, that in the development of an economy, the education of the general public is as important as that of a skilled work-force because it determines the general attitude to what is desirable as well as the disciplines and restrictions which will be accepted in the effort to attain it.

This point is so important today in Britain and, indeed, in most European countries, that it deserves elaboration. It is certain that more resources are being devoted than can be afforded to the study of subjects and activities having little or no industrial importance and contributing not at all to national prosperity. Furthermore, powerful and age-hallowed institutions, such as the older universities and the 'Public' schools, contain within themselves elements which are gravely prejudicial to the public welfare. As a result of their operation, talent is led away from science and technology towards studies having only traditional reputability, while resources are expended for the upkeep of useless posts and buildings at the cost of those upon which survival depends. The problems arising from the complex relations set up within modern industry are ignored. The reasons for the fall of ancient empires are studied, those that might lead to the decay of modern societies are avoided. Traditional disciplines are revered, technology is considered unworthy of real university status. Degrees are granted to those who specialize for a few years in modern or ancient languages, and refused to others of equal ability who devote themselves to less reputable but more useful aspects of human activity, calling for just as high a degree of ability. Blind tradition, operating through outworn institutions, blocks the path to progress and creates troubles which cannot be understood or dealt with. In spite of all that has been said recently about the imperative need for trained scientists and technologists, the idea still prevails in England that at least as many university students should be trained in the 'liberal arts' as in the sciences – as if there was an endless reservoir of high talent and as if there was something sacred and absolute in these 'fair shares'.

Under-developed countries illustrate the same principles just as clearly. Many nations claim to want the material benefits of technology but are unwilling to pay the social price which would make its adoption possible. A Muslim nation may want the material benefits of the factory system, but be unwilling to utilize its women as factory labour. Yet it can be demonstrated that such a society cannot compete with a Western society which utilizes all its population. A South American nation may dream of the material advantages of industrialization, but be unwilling to abandon the security and the comfort of a semi-feudal system. Such attitudes may in the long run be more significant for national economy than the direct training of labour. It is fairly easy to teach a man from the most primitive of societies basic skills which, when brought together in the carefully organized pattern of large-scale industry, lead to the fabrication of steel, the weaving of textiles, the refining of oil, and the operation of railways and airlines. The development of the managerial skills needed to organize these simpler skills and to guide the enormously complex enterprise of modern industry can also be developed, though with much greater difficulty, by formal education and extended experience. But all this will count for naught if the society itself in which the new industries operate is not adequately prepared for them. Lack of social and political cohesion among the population of France may well bring disaster, in spite of the intelligence of its leaders and the technical skill and inventiveness of its people. The rapid recovery of Germany after World War II is the reward for the willing acceptance of the disciplines of industrial life, although the reverse of the medal – political docility – was the condition for the disasters that overwhelmed her. The amazing wealth and expanding economy of the U.S.A. come not merely from the vast natural resources: indeed, the modern frontier and the untapped wealth are in the laboratories and in the minds of its people. Yet not all the training of its industrial army nor the education and experience of its managers could explain its success. The deepest roots of this expansion lie in a national attitude of daring and in a continuing optimism in the possibilities of the future – though doubt and strain may worsen the ulcers and thromboses produced by wrong feeding.

Once again we are led to the view that it is society's attitude to education, the institutionalized expressions of its social philosophy, which determine the way in which its schools contribute to economic well-being.

Five Types of Attitude towards the Support of Education

1 Education as a human right

When considering typical national attitudes towards the purposes of education, one comes across five basic patterns. The first is also the most novel and most popular. It has been consecrated in the Bill of Human Rights prepared by the United Nations and assumes that every human being on earth, by the mere fact of birth, has a right to be educated just as he has an absolute and inalienable right to life, liberty, the pursuit of happiness, and – some would add – the enjoyment of private property. What Jeremy Bentham would have said about this new 'natural and inalienable right' can well be imagined – in any case, the ideal it expresses is probably unattainable and perhaps unreasonable. Our purpose here is not to argue this point but rather to suggest that, even if education *per se* is a good thing, too much even of a good thing may do ill. This is true for education, although most Americans would hate to admit it. It seems almost certain that modern techniques of education can develop the potential qualities of many individuals in a society to a degree so high that few societies, if any, can adequately absorb the talent produced. It is all very well to argue that widespread non-functional education merely serves to give the society a high cultural level. In fact, however, with the increased educational level, there comes an increase in 'felt needs' and social demands, which the society cannot supply. Inevitably there comes 'unemployment', social unrest, and individual frustration. The country of Lebanon has for fifty years developed more talent through education than its economy can absorb, and the only solution has been to export population – not the poor and uneducated immigrants with which the Western world is familiar, but the highest cultural products of that society. This is obviously a fantastic economic and social loss. The new country of Israel is also an example of too high a concentration of education in an economy unable to support it. Using scientists and scholars with doctoral degrees as simple labourers in the development of the Negev may provide dramatic propaganda, but it is hardly an economic utilization of manpower. No society operating such a system can be stable.

2 Education as an indispensable service

In the U.S.A. and, to a varying degree, in other advanced countries it is widely held that a society cannot afford less education than the maximum it is able to finance. Superficially convincing proofs, some of a negative kind, are adduced. It is clear, for instance, that both in

E

Britain and in the U.S.A., there are dismaying shortages of techni-cally competent manpower. Official reports have been published in both countries which stress the gap between need and supply. The really disturbing shortage of teachers of science and mathematics is deplored: the long-range implications on the future training of en-gineers is evident. It seems, too, that only about half the personnel required is being produced, and that many large plants have hundreds of posts which they cannot fill. Furthermore, about half of all college or university graduates are needed to staff the schools. Yet, in the U.S.A., only 20 per cent have actually been entering teaching. Ameri-cans estimate that the need for new university teachers during the next ten or fifteen years will far surpass the total number of doctoral degrees awarded in that period. The quality of instruction must therefore inevitably fall: by 1970 only 20 per cent of college teachers will have a Ph.D. degree, instead of the 40 per cent who now hold it. Similarly, it is extremely doubtful whether the new English higher technological colleges, on the building of which vast sums are to be spent, will be able to recruit adequate numbers of competent teachers. It seems that both countries have in the past invested too little in higher education and that they are now to pay the price of neglect. What is known about the training of scientific and technolo-logical personnel in the Soviet Union highlights the situation and gives it dramatic urgency.

Another superficially convincing proof put forward is that the U.S.A. is the richest nation on earth and that it has the highest general level of education; the two facts being causally related. Some observers, of course, have doubts about the quality of American education. This is a matter of judgement and of values. But no one can challenge the statistical facts that the United States has over-whelmingly the highest concentration of secondary school graduates, with twelve years or more of formal education, of college gradu-ates, with sixteen or more years of formal education, and of persons holding standard doctoral degrees, representing nineteen or more years of formal education. The United States has 1,806 recognized institutions of higher learning, comparable to universities or inde-pendent university colleges in Europe. For the past five years Amer-ican college enrolment has been running at approximately two and a half million. It is estimated that between 1966 and 1971 this enrolment is likely to be doubled. Even the so-called depressed minorities among the American population have educational benefits far surpassing that of any other nation on earth. Thus, the Negroes have a substantially higher percentage of university graduates than that of any European nation.

It would be easy, therefore, to draw the conclusion that America's income is largely or solely the result of this very high concentration of educational investment. There is certainly a correlation between a nation's income and its educational investment, but it is not a simple one. The United States could not possibly have achieved, nor could it maintain, its economy without very large investments in education, but it does not at all follow that this is the sole or even the dominant reason. During a period when the national income has expanded by about five, the expenditure on education has expanded by less than 50 per cent, and this with no adjustment for the inflation which has approximately doubled the cost of living. The explanation, of course, is in part the lag between the educational investment and the resultant change in national economy. America, like England, is living on the educational investment of twenty years ago, and the predicted manpower – and hence industrial – difficulties in the next ten years can be directly traced to a failure in educational policy during and immediately after World War II.

3 Education creates élites

Traditionally, the French, and to a lesser degree the English, think of education, especially at the higher level, as something intended for a small and select group. Qualities of mind are thought to be the essential requirement for leadership: the wise should lead and wisdom comes from the right education. This view is supported in part by simple traditional reverence and in part by an appeal to the outworn psychological theory of 'formal discipline'. The French, for instance, argue that intensive study produces a toughening of the mind analogous to the strengthening of muscles through exercise. They hold that the study of languages and mathematics is 'good', whether or not these subjects will be used. The English argument is slightly different: it is the view that the qualities of character and personality needed to lead men are developed through contact with the liberal and humane disciplines, through literature, language, philosophy,

history, and that it is essential to develop a proper misunderstanding
of the role and function of science by continually pointing out its
'limitations'. Here one perceives the importance of the Platonic
illusion that men can know absolute truth – an illusion which denies
to man the supreme satisfaction of struggling to escape other illusions.

All these beliefs are linked to another myth, namely that somehow
there should be restrictions on numbers receiving higher education if
the quality of the latter is to be maintained as well as the social position of those who have enjoyed its benefits. In order to achieve this
double aim, a complicated system of barriers, in the form of examinations, has been established. Candidates pass or are rejected on the
basis of an almost savage elimination of those who fail to meet arbitrary standards. In principle, these standards should be deliberately
adjusted so that society would receive precisely the number of doctors, lawyers, engineers, professors, chemists, and so on that the
economy needs. This would involve being able to forecast future
needs accurately, and agreeing upon the type of society desired. In
point of fact, what happens is that society receives an alarming number of defeated frustrates, while the way in which both France and
England stagger from one economic and financial crisis to another,
hampered dreadfully by shortage of trained manpower, dramatizes
the inaccuracy of forecasting and the failure of foresight.

The application of the *élite* theory to other areas of social organization has produced interesting phenomena. One of these is the 'down-
ward filtration' theory in colonialism. If the leader should be that
one who is distinguished by intellectual or educational or social
attainments, it naturally follows that the best method of raising the
cultural standards of colonial areas is to educate leaders and allow
them to raise the standards of the masses of their people. The technical success and the political chaos which this system has produced are
only too painfully apparent in many areas of the world.

The economic result of this educational policy is extensive and
evident. It has produced an economic class-society with built-in limits
on the development of purchasing power of the masses, with a clear-
cut hierarchy of economic power, and with a dangerous inherent
antagonism between management and labour. It fails to develop an
adequate reserve of talent which could be made available for rapid

economic growth and for adjustment to rapidly changing conditions. It tends to reward intellectualism and hence, unfortunately, verbalism, while it tends to disregard practical skills and individual initiative. It lays stress on stability and individual security, and develops a large class of civil service bureaucrats and inflexible workers in an undynamic economy resistant to change.

4 Education as thought-control

The concept of education as a centrally controlled instrument for manipulating the minds of a people goes back to the ancient world, but has been illustrated by the practices of the Italian Fascists, the Nazis, the militarists of Japan, and the communists. The system of schools and universities serves as a selective valve through which flows only the kinds of knowledge and skill which the ruling groups consider good. In its less objectionable form this is not very different from the control of education by religious organizations, so that the religious but uninstructed believers will not be confused or led astray by intellectually superior non-believers. In its most vicious and amoral forms it leads to brain-washing and regimentation. Somewhere in between, education has consciously or unconsciously been used by all societies as an instrument of economic and social control.

We pride ourselves, for example, on 'consumer courses' in which we attempt to teach values and judgement in the appraisal and purchase of material or cultural goods. We develop a subtle attitude towards taste, economic values, and even towards the products offered in our markets. Thus, the smell of flowers or musk has social status, while the odour of onions or garlic requires masking by chlorophyll. We teach that ownership of a house implies one set of social standards, while ownership of a television or a refrigerator or a motorcar has another. There can be no denying that education of this sort conveys real benefits by achieving the kind of society which a people desire, but the line between education and propaganda, between learning and advertising, between political consciousness and regimentation, is a very difficult one to draw. There can be little doubt that in the freest of societies man is easily susceptible to the development of an uncritical submissiveness to mass opinion. We follow the fads and fashions of our times in political ideas as well as in clothing.

5 Education for national development

The last of the five typical patterns of social attitudes towards education is that which considers it the tool *par excellence* for achieving national unity as well as for technological development. For instance, the leaders of under-developed societies argue that 'the great nations of the world are great because they have available trained leadership and skilled personnel. If we have the same, we can develop our own country, utilize our resources, and achieve our rightful position in the world's community of nations.'

The concept of education as the essential element for national development is based in part on a recognition of the status and prestige of those who do have education and who live within the underdeveloped area. Even a relatively modest degree of education sets the individual apart. In addition there exists a belief that education is directly correlated with political, economic, and social power. Finally, this belief is based on the idea that only lack of education stands in the way of technological and economic development. The individual who has already achieved status through education, but aspires to greatness both for himself and for his people, tends to forget that the powerful and rich nations of the world have an accumulation of experience and of capital, together with powerful alliances and economic links with societies and markets which only a long history can provide.

The example of Iran makes this quite clear. That country has enjoyed a relatively high level of educational opportunity for the past thirty years. There exists in its population a large body of personnel with advanced university degrees from distinguished institutions in Europe and the United States. Iran has one of the best systems of technical schools and, proportionately, one of the largest systems of secondary schools, in the Middle East. It has a national university and several faculties of a second university. Yet Iran has been unable to absorb its existing trained personnel. In 1949 a census showed that there were approximately fourteen thousand university graduates who were not practising their professions and who could not be located in the general population. One of the major problems which has faced the oil industry, both before and after nationalization, has been the crippling necessity of maintaining on the pay-roll very large numbers of technical personnel for whom there is no real need and no economic justification. As long as such a situation exists, far from being beneficial, education tends to depress the economy and to create a potentially explosive social situation. It will be extremely difficult, if not impossible, for Iran's major industry, oil, to compete in free world markets if it must carry the heavy burden of continued employment of trained but unnecessary personnel. Yet it is equally difficult, from a political and social point of view, to leave unemployed this surplus of technical personnel. It may well be questioned whether other existing or potential industries in Iran can in the foreseeable future absorb the excess. In such circumstances a drive to increase educational opportunity can certainly be seriously questioned.

Not all under-developed areas have basic restrictions such as those of Iran, however. Brazil, for example, has such unlimited possibilities for population growth, and such enormous natural resources, that there is likely to be almost an unlimited market for trained personnel at any time in the foreseeable future. Where intensive education in an under-developed area might very well produce an over-supply of trained personnel in certain industries or regions, the very size and potential richness of Brazil, together with its diversified pattern of industries, make possible an almost infinite number of readjustments so that it is unlikely that a situation like that in Iran could arise.

The United States can hardly be called an under-developed area. Yet the very rate of change and the speed of its growth have indicated that national development is entirely a relative matter. The U.S.A. represents an outstanding example of what Brazil may become through investment in education and industry. One of the major reasons for the constant need for education and training, in a nation which already has such a high level of educational attainment, is precisely the fact that a dynamic economic system rapidly makes skills obsolescent and produces serious dislocation in the employment of the work-force. It is estimated that the average industrial worker in the United States must be retrained every six or seven years, because of technological changes. This is possible only if the work-force originally possesses a relatively high level of general education. The difficulty is overcome only through an enormous annual expenditure, much of it hidden and contributed by the industries themselves in constant retraining of personnel.

Policy and Management of Resources

Against the background of societal attitudes – such as we have described above – those who control education frame their policy. That is to say, they decide how to acquire resources, how to allocate them, and how to administer them efficiently. Today, all these problems are couched in terms of finance. It should be noted, however, that peculiar problems arise in societies changing quickly from the old barter economies towards those based on money. The transitional period is a difficult one. Once tribal or family living begins to break down, services in kind and the functional social organization of work tend to be replaced by wage structures, and consumer goods are bought for money. More important, social organization tends to be determined economically with entrepreneurs distorting the general pattern of the efficient use of resources. Non-essential goods are often produced, if there is a sale for them from which profit is derived – which profit is not necessarily reinvested in society. Personnel no longer work in occupations in which, in a vague sense, they are most 'useful' socially; very often they are encouraged to move into better-paid occupations which benefit the few rather than the many. The criteria of guidance, selection, and maintaining personnel in various jobs change. Time, accommodation, high social prestige, and status can no longer be set aside for people fulfilling useful functions as they were in small self-supporting societies. If there is a demand for certain kinds of skill, other incentives have to be found to attract them and other resources placed at their disposal.

The transition from one kind of economy to another involves changing from one source of 'wealth' to another in acquiring resources for any service – and for education. In primitive and preindustrial societies the sources of wealth were land and property. Many educational systems have been created and maintained on these. It is necessary to look only at the church schools and the land-grant colleges in the United States to recognize this.

As the economy changes so do the criteria of evaluating the services provided. In a money economy an education which leads to a better-paid job is likely to be valued highly. Social evaluations on the desirability of this or that kind of education are extremely difficult to make. Even correlations between national productivity or national income and education are not easy to draw. Let us turn once more to advanced societies. It has been said already that the policy maker is concerned, in the first place, with the search for resources. Here, three questions immediately arise. The first is <u>whether the sources to be tapped are reputable.</u> Some money is socially unacceptable in most societies, as for example, the returns on gambling, taxes on liquor, licence fees on prostitutes. Certain money is socially acceptable in many societies but unacceptable in some, as for example, money from religious sources, federal funds for equalization of opportunity, and foreign aid. And some funds are acceptable everywhere, as for example, individual tuition fees and local taxation.

Closely linked with all this is the problem of side-effects resulting from drawing on such income. In the United States, for example, most people would welcome federal funds to assist education, yet for a wide variety of reasons probably a majority are unwilling to accept them – because of fear of racial miscegenation, the possibility of religious influence, the fear of federal control, the possibility of excessively high taxes, local fear of a flight of capital, the possibility of slums and blighted areas, and so on.

Whatever the current or local attitudes, almost all societies finance education from six basic sources. These are: <u>credit in the form of municipal or district bonds or loans; taxes or rates, including tax benefits such as exemptions for non-profit and philanthropic agencies; tuition or individual payment for educational services; profits arising from the sale of goods and services produced directly or indirectly by the educational institutions; income from endowment or other productive investments; and non-recurring income from gifts, charity, or bequests.</u>

The second major problem in financing is that of the management of expenditures. Here, there is inevitably a conflict between 'efficiency' and 'effectiveness'. In earlier and less sophisticated times, business managers tended to measure efficiency in terms of *per capita* and unit costs. This is obviously misleading, if not meaningless, since <u>education is efficient only if it is effective, and the measurement of effectiveness is not a financial but primarily a social matter.</u> The educational system of pre-war Japan, for example, was one of the most efficient in the world from the point of view of *per capita* expenditure. It might even be considered efficient from the point of view of immediate and superficial attainment – such as the degree of literacy or the percentage of the population who attained secondary and higher levels. But seen historically, Japan's educational system was a catastrophic failure, for it produced a regimented, docile population which was duped by its leaders and led to defeat and disaster.

In the management of expenditure, methods of accounting inevitably influence cost. Skill in drawing up budgets and forecasts (either dividing up the available money or doing the job regardless of ultimate expense) basically affect the efficiency. Audit, appraisal, and control of the actual finances of a school or system are certainly important in maintaining accuracy and accountability. In all this, educational finance is no different from any other type – whether government, industrial, or personal – except in the evaluation of results.

Perhaps the major obstacle to developing a good appraisal system for education is the time-lag which inevitably exists. The effects of an educational procedure are seldom immediately apparent. Johnny may not learn to read and this, in a gross sense, is a condemnation of the quality of the education he has received. But in most educational systems Johnny *does* learn to read, and the real test of whether his education was 'good' or not is determined only much later in life when one can see what Johnny does with his reading. Failure to learn some skills is dramatically more apparent in some cases than in others. Thus, a poorly trained navigator or pilot crashes his plane, and a poorly trained surgeon or physician kills his patient. But the difference in the life pattern of Johnny, whether he is well or poorly trained in reading or in social attitudes, may take a generation to become apparent, and the result may even then not be closely identified with the cause.

There is also the difficulty of comparing intangibles. What is an attitude worth in comparison to a skill? There were few societies in the world with more highly developed skills than Nazi Germany, yet the failure to develop proper attitudes led to the greatest catastrophe the world has yet seen. There is the problem of relative values. In every society and economy, long-range changes take place which are difficult to evaluate and which may not become apparent for so long a time that modification of the educational system is difficult or impossible. Thus, for example, through education a man may gain life and lose his soul – he may improve his material well-being but abandon worthy ethical standards. Even some of the characteristics presumably most desirable over a short range of time may prove to be disastrous in the end. Thus, in the free world there are few who would deny that individualism and the willingness to stand against the crowd are desirable characteristics, yet this very characteristic has proved disruptive to French society. On the other hand, we may laud teamplay and the subordination of one's personal interest to the good of the group, yet this led to regimentation and to the enslavement of the individual in Nazi Germany.

Another important question is the effect of education on the total economy. This has received far less attention and is probably less susceptible to accurate research than simple matters of educational finance. By its very nature, it must be studied in terms of indirect results.

It was earlier noted that the productive pattern of any economy depends upon capital, raw materials, transportation, managerial skill, and trained labour. The relative importance in any single organization of the trained work-force and of the consumer is an indirect measure of educational attainment. Three examples will suffice to illustrate this. The first is that of mechanization, and especially of automation. Whether the change takes place as a result or as a cause of an educational endeavour, it is nevertheless certain that education will be a major limiting factor upon the extent and the success of such an organization of work. Without high levels of education, some forms of organization are not possible.

A second example is that of technological development. One of the tragic mistakes which most under-developed nations make is in their belief that because they can learn successfully to operate an existing industry, they have in fact achieved the ability to compete in that industry. Nothing could be further from the truth – because the success and survival of industry in the modern world depend upon the dynamic qualities of continued and intensive industrial research, and most industries become obsolescent and non-competitive almost immediately unless supported by such researches. Obviously scientific research cannot be carried on without an adequate educational system.

A third example is the development of consumer attitudes, again a highly specialized but nevertheless an extremely important element in the economic effects of education. In 1954 one of the three most powerful automobile corporations in America faced serious economic reverses because it was unable accurately either to gauge or to modify public taste. In the following year it almost completely reversed its disadvantageous economic position by successfully meeting these two needs. On three occasions major British aeronautical companies suffered the dismaying economic consequences of inadequate engineering. In each case the deficiency in engineering was ultimately corrected, but the loss to the economy could not be recouped so readily. In one case the prototype of an aircraft had to be removed from service; in another, failure of a wing structure delayed the utilization of the model until the design was approaching obsolescence; and in the third case, Britain lost her unchallenged position in the jet-propulsion field. It would be inaccurate to state that education was responsible for the immediate errors or omissions of the engineers who were concerned. But it can be argued that lack of an adequate body of trained engineers and technicians limited the amount of research and testing, and hence delayed the successful building of acceptable models. Germany in World War II suffered from this same lack of trained personnel as a result of its educational system. That country could not adequately man five major programmes simultaneously – radar, submarines, guided missiles, jet propulsion, and atomic fission.

The indirect and intangible results of education have enormous effects upon any economy. It is a popular pastime for Europeans and Asians to laugh at the American preoccupation with bathrooms, television sets, cars, and refrigerators. Yet no one can deny that the economy of the United States might collapse and bring economic ruin to all the world if a chain reaction were set up in which its public lost interest in canned and frozen foods, Sunday afternoon drives, the sacred daily bath, and the favourite T.V. comedian. These tastes and attitudes are inextricably linked with the economic organization of society. Complex economies run on intangibles – attractive packaging, recognition trim on new models, a preference for certain trade names and brands, and the presumed necessity of using special types of soaps and powders, toothpaste, and cigarettes if one's health and allure and professional competence are to be preserved. Even the stern and politically generated attitudes towards economic life common among European nations are based not alone on simple patriotic slogans and propaganda, but also have their roots deep in the lives of the people and the bringing-up of their children. The Germans were induced to accept guns instead of butter as much by the schools as by the political orator. England's austerity with 'fair shares for all' came as much from school-inspired ethics of good sportsmanship as it did from party programmes and political editorials. It would be a mistake to think that America's economy rests solely on the skills of the radio huckster and of the advertising man. It stems fundamentally from a national conviction in the possibility of an expanding economy, which is one of the fundamental characteristics of American life.

The third measurable effect of investment in education is that provided by the growth of national income. Such a measure has many limitations. It is an attempt to correlate a complex end-result of many interlocking factors, with a single one of those factors. It has the limitation of measuring only one of the effects – the material one – out of a large number of observable results from the educational endeavour. It has the disadvantage that a time-lag exists between the investment and the national profit. And, above all, it suffers because the relationship between educational investment and resultant national income is so complex that it seems almost impossible to establish precise statistical results. With all these limitations, the fact remains that a correlation between educational investment and national income does exist, and, in rough terms can probably be determined. Such a measure of the effectiveness of an educational system has a very real attractiveness to many people. In their individual lives they are willing to accept this measure regardless of its imperfections. Parents make sacrifices and youth invests its best years in an educational investment which they know offers the greatest single chance for economic as well as social benefit.

BIBLIOGRAPHY

Anderson, C. Arnold and Bowman, Mary Jean (editors). *Education and Economic Development*. London, Cass, 1966. x, 436 pp.

The following four areas are developed historically, geographically, economically, sociologically, and educationally: the analysis of investment in human resource formation and its contributions to the economy; the analysis of processes and loss of the formation of human competencies; the analysis of patterns and processes in the diffusion of schooling, technologies and educational opportunity; an historical survey of the preconditions for development and change.

Benson, Charles S. *The Economics of Public Education*. Boston, Houghton Mifflin, 1961. xx, 580 pp.

Basic economic analysis is applied to a comprehensive selection of topics in the financing of education. Major sources for school revenue, and problems of school expenditure in the United States are analysed in detail.

Blaug, M. *Economics of Education: A Selected Annotated Bibliography*. (International series of monographs in *Library and Information Science*, Volume 3) Oxford, Pergamon, 1966. xiii 190 pp.

An annotated list of about 800 published items in English, French, German and a large number of unpublished yet obtainable items. Three addenda in stencilled form (obtainable from the author) bring the bibliography up to date to January 1968.

D'Hoogh, Christian. *Problèmes Economiques de l'Enseignement: Contribution à l'etude de l'Investissement en Capital Humaine.* Brussels, Centre d'Etude des Problèmes Sociaux et Professionnels de la Technique, 1963. viii, 221 pp.

A comprehensive account of the relationship between economics and education in Belgium is preceded by a short discussion of Schultz's, Edding's and Vaizey's work.

Hanson, John W. and Brembeck, Cole S. *Education and the Development of Nations.* New York/London, Holt, Rinehart and Winston, 1966. xiv, 529 pp.

This book describes the kind of functionally planned education required for constructive social, political and economic development.

OECD Study Group in the Economics of Education. *Financing of Education for Economic Growth*: Papers prepared for the conference organized by the Directorate of Scientific Affairs of OECD, Paris 1964. Paris, OECD, no date. 429 pp.

The first part deals with the specific problems of finance in developing countries, and in the second part the techniques used to establish national educational budgets and to finance their budgets in OECD member countries are described. Student, state and local financing is dealt with, and forecasts of financial implications of educational expansion is given.

Policy Conference on Economic Growth and Investment in Education. Washington, 1961. Paris, OECD, 1963.

Five papers include sections on: targets for education in Europe; the challenge of aid to newly developing countries; the planning of education in relation to economic growth, the international flows of students.

Robinson E. A. G. and Vaizey, J. E. (editors). *The Economics of Education*: proceedings of a conference held by the International Economic Association. London, Macmillan, 1966. xvii, 781 pp.

National expenditures on education are compared; education is seen as a means of promoting economic growth; the demand and supply for education, the cost, finance and measurement of cost and finance of education, the balanced planning of education and international aid to education are subjects covered in this comprehensive work.

Schultz, Theodore W. *The Economic Value of Education*. New York/ London, Columbia University Press, 1963. xii, 92 pp.
One of the leading contributors to the subject reviews past work and future research opportunities. The basic hypothesis is that the economic value of education depends predominantly on the demand for, and the supply of, schooling approached as an investment.

Sinha, M. R. (editor) *The Economics of Manpower Planning*. Bombay, Asian Studies Press for Indian Institute of Asian Studies, 1965. xii, 194 pp.
The economic aspects of manpower planning in educational development in Japan and Hungary are presented in a symposium as examples which provide a theoretical view of the problem.

Unesco. *Readings in the Economics of Education*: a selection of articles, essays and texts from the works of economists, past and present, on the relationships between economics and education. Paris, Unesco, 1968. 945 pp.
All aspects are covered: planning, resources, development, costs in benefits, content and locus of education for economic benefit, measures of the contribution of schooling to per capita income growth.

Vaizey, John. *The Costs of Education*. London, Allen and Unwin 1958. 256 pp.
An authoritative review of United Kingdom expenditure on education from 1920–1955, documenting the 'surprisingly meagre flow of resources into education'.

Educational Planning

from the 1967 World Year Book of Education
George Z. F. Bereday
Joseph A. Lauwerys

By focusing on planning the 1967 *Year Book* follows a tradition well established in Comparative Education. Men like Victor Cousin in France, Matthew Arnold in England, Horace Mann in the U.S.A. paid close attention to foreign educational systems when preparing schemes for the orderly development of their own. An interest in the economic dimension, too, is nothing new. There were *Year Books* on *Education and Economics* in 1956 and on *Education and Technological Development* in 1954. Since then great progress has been made and interest continues to grow. As evidence, a few examples will suffice: the foundation of the International Institute in Paris, of the Research Unit at the University of London Institute of Education, of the Higher Education Unit at the London School of Economics and the work being done at Columbia, Chicago, Indiana, the Max Planck Institute in Berlin.

By drawing together into one volume contributions from many distinguished specialists, it was our hope to be of help in the necessary organization and systematization of a field which is full of promise. At a time when the demand for access to education everywhere grows tremendously, it is obvious that the scarce resources should be stretched to their maximum effectiveness. Moreover, the needs of technological and industrializing societies impose the necessity for matching educational output with professional manpower requirements. So the practical applications of educational planning are of evident importance.

There are, too, exceedingly interesting theoretical considerations. Some educators argue that planning tends to treat men as replaceable cogs in a giant machine and that it deflects attention from the centrality of the human person and his needs in education. There are sociologists who point out that thinking too much about overall planning may lead to the creation of a technocratic *élite* and thus divide the population into the managers and the managed, the former not always using their powers with wisdom and justice. Then, too, there is the 'cybernetic' argument that planning cannot possibly take into account the multitudinous and involved activities of a complex and rapidly changing society and that elasticity of intention and swiftness of performance rather than planning lead to success in modern industrial enterprises. Such views deserve respect: there is at least some truth in them. How does one reconcile planning and freedom? Can one really, as Karl Mannheim said, plan for freedom?

Part I

Mark Blaug
Joseph A. Lauwerys

It has been said that the earliest example of comprehensive planning in education is to be found in the *Republic* where Plato proposes a well-articulated scheme which takes account of the political needs of the city state – as he saw them – and which makes the school the servant of society. The history of education provides many other instances. John Knox, in the sixteenth century (*c.* 1560), described a national system of schools and colleges which would serve the Scots and lead them not only to spiritual salvation but to material well-being. A few decades later, Comenius explained in much detail how schools should be organized and run in order to cement national unity and cohesion.

As science and industry became more complex, so did the schemes of educational planners. Influenced no doubt by the Encyclopaedists and the Physiocrats, La Chalotais (1763) suggested in some detail the establishment of a nationalized system of elementary education, dealing with all the children of all the people, and intended to teach them useful, positive knowledge. Rousseau, at about the same time, advised the Poles to take measures to build schools and provide teaching for all citizens: his ideas were down to earth and realistic. He even included advice as to when to inflict corporal punishment on unsatisfactory pupils who did not work hard enough.

The notion of planned education on a national scale appealed to the Benevolent Despots and it was not long before the outlines began to take practical shape: during the first half of the nineteenth century, the Prussian authorities, for instance, built schools and trained teachers in advance of existing demand, guessing how that demand might grow.

It would, however, be mistaken to press too far the argument that there is nothing new in the idea of educational planning. There are profound differences between schemes like the above and those studied by the educational planners of today. The aims pursued, of course, are not the same: the preparation of efficient technicians instead of brave soldiers or obedient citizens. But this is only the acceptance of other purposes. The true novelty is in the methodology employed, with its reliance on advanced and refined modes of analysis. The new planning has the same kind of relation to the old as the design and planning methods of a giant automobile factory have to the work of an eighteenth-century coach maker. The difference in the size and complexity of the enterprise is so great that quantity passes into quality. A new kind of activity has come into existence. Engineering blue-prints are being prepared instead of pleasing impressionistic drawings.

One feature that seems new is in fact not as new as is often believed; the reliance upon the views of economists and upon techniques used in business management. Adam Smith was certainly not alone among eighteenth-century economists in taking an interest in education and, of course, Alfred Marshall devoted several chapters in his *Principles of Economics* (1891) to education and industrial training. Administrators of school systems have long learnt lessons from the management of industrial and commercial enterprises. The monitorial system, to mention but one illustration, was an application to the classroom of methods employed in the factory. In a profoundly interesting book,[1] Raymond E. Callahan shows that in the first few decades of the century, great pressure was brought to bear upon American educational administrators by commercial and industrial groups. They were persuaded, even forced, to operate schools in accordance with the managerial techniques of the period. They adopted business values and followed the edicts of the time and motion study experts. The principals of schools accepted the role of business executives or plant managers. Callahan concluded that this cult of 'efficiency' led to an undermining of intellectual standards. He deplores the fact that even today the questions often asked, even by teachers and educationists, are of the type. 'How can we operate our schools to produce more engineers, mathematicians and scientists?' rather than 'How can we provide an excellent education for our children?'

National Plans

We may sympathize with Callahan's views and take warning from what happened to the well-meant efforts of our predecessors when they were led away from the pursuit of broad and generous educational aims. Yet, at the same time, we should be ready to admit that one aspect of any educational system is that it is a machine designed to produce given results (for instance, to teach young people the mastery of particular skills of hand and mind). If it is a machine, it should be efficient; it should run smoothly without undue waste. If manpower can be economized, it should be.

These arguments are fully accepted, of course, by all planners. But there is more to the general notion of 'planning in education' as it is understood today. The educational system of a country is linked closely and organically to the whole production process just as it is to the political and to the social environment. In earlier times, this point was frequently overlooked, partly because apprenticeship tended to be seen as an alternative to schooling; an alternative, moreover, which was not an integral part of real education. When production of material goods, however, depends as largely as it does upon the contribution of specialists in the basic and applied sciences and upon the careful and skilled work of well-educated technicians, the

[1] *Education and the Cult of Efficiency*, Chicago: 1962.

relationship of education to production becomes evident to all. Universities and technical colleges are now among the chief sources of trained manpower. They contribute directly to the general increase in wealth. Modern industry, moreover, is everywhere very closely related to what happens in every sector of the life of nations. A dispute among railway workers, itself arising from trivial causes, can bring to a standstill an automobile factory or a canning plant a thousand miles away. A political decision taken in Washington can affect the building industry of Southern California. A strike in the Port of London can bring unemployment to textile workers in the North of England. Shortage of skilled electricians can hamper the development of an important industry. Modern life is highly integrated.

One consequence is that educational planning must now, of necessity, be at least national in scope. The 1944 Education Act in England made it mandatory for each of the 146 local education authorities to prepare a development plan to be submitted to the central Ministry of Education. Many of these plans are quite remarkably far-sighted. Predictions about the numbers of pupils likely to attend the different kinds of schools form the basis for building plans. The location of schools is studied in relation to the growth and movement of population. Attempts to forecast the growth of industries and the building of new factories are taken into account. Estimates of the yield of local taxation for many years ahead are presented. Tentative budgets are included. Forecasts of the numbers of teachers needed to staff the schools are contrasted with the likely output of training colleges. In fact, everything that can possibly be done by skilled and devoted administrators is included in these impressive plans – most of which, incidentally, remain largely unrealized because of continuing financial and economic difficulties, or to put the matter in another way, because the English people chose not to accord to education quite as high a degree of priority as educational enthusiasts would like.

It is now understood and accepted that local plans of this kind no longer suffice. The forecasts and projections upon which they rest have to deal with whole countries, if only because modern populations are geographically mobile.

In addition, of course, planning itself, as a concept, has become popular and respected. It was probably the U.S.S.R. that first used it as a basis of policy. The Bolsheviks rejected the notions of free enterprise and of a free market, considering them as only devices for exploiting the proletariat and robbing the masses. The making of profit was considered immoral. But entrepreneurs decide what to produce and how much by taking account of likely profits. How then was industry and the economy of the Soviet States to be guided and directed? Planning seemed the socialist answer, planning the production of goods to satisfy human needs rather than to maximize profits. And so came a succession of Five-Year Plans and a spectacular development of industry and technology. Planning seemed to get results and it looked as though it helped to avoid waste by allocating wisely and prudently both human and material resources.

But it is not only in socialist states that the idea of planning has gained ground. As the size of industrial enterprises grows, it becomes evident that a great number of factors have to be taken into account and correlated if the whole is to function smoothly: raw materials have to be ordered years in advance, subsidiary factories built, sources of electrical power developed, labour trained and so on. Think, for example, of the astoundingly complicated organizational web needed to run, say a large oil combine or an aircraft industry. Overall planning, far sighted and comprehensive, dealing with many thousands of workers, is an absolute necessity. Planning in fact, is not simply a device favoured by socialists but an ideologically neutral instrument which has to be used in all really large-scale enterprises – and a national education system certainly is a large-scale enterprise employing many thousands and using expensive plant.

Educational Plans

To plan the development of an educational system is in many ways a more hazardous and difficult matter than to plan, say, the development of an automobile industry. The aims are far less clear: it is not simply a question of making an even larger number of a limited range of vehicles at a continuously falling price. Since education is not bought and sold in a market, it is not clear what criteria are to be applied to measure the adequacy of an educational system. How much education should be provided and what is the correct balance between different types of education?

Here it is well to note that, quite often in science, it is not necessary to measure directly: an index related to whatever one is interested in may be a useful indicator. No doctor really wants to know how hot the patient's body is: but temperature may indicate how ill he is. So, too, it is possible that indicators may be found which give information regarding the soundness of an educational system and which may help to determine the direction in which it should develop. Those who have specialized in the study of educational planning during the last dozen years, in fact, tend to pay attention to three main kinds of indicators which are described critically in the 1967 *Year Book*. First comes the social-demand approach, of which the (British) Robbins Report on Higher Education is a splendid example. Attempts are made to forecast the future demand for places, taking account of demographic and social trends. The assumption is made that the provision of more education will of necessity benefit the economy so that the additional costs will not prove too heavy a burden. Consumer choice is given wide scope, partly because it is difficult to force young people to study subjects in which they are not interested and partly because it is exceedingly hard to forecast five or ten years in advance what kinds of training will be needed in a rapidly changing economy. It is evident that this approach commends itself to those who favour a permissive social climate, who are attached to traditional cultural values and who work in societies where public opinion has great influence.

Next comes the manpower-requirements approach. Here the fundamental idea is that total production should grow as fast as possible, even if this involves some limitation of personal choice. Modern production needs educated workers trained in the right skills. Is it possible to estimate ten years in advance how much of each kind of skill a country will be able to employ? If so, how can the manpower be allocated and trained? The difficulty, of course, is that new kinds of industry continually come into existence and new kinds of specialisms are needed. The danger is that the aims pursued may be so narrow as to be self-defeating. Nevertheless this approach recommends itself in part because it leads rather quickly to the employment of quantitative data and in part because it stresses the employment aspects of education which are often overlooked.

The cost-benefit approach, on the other hand, is a direct one: work out the costs of various types of education and compare them with the returns, both to the individual and to society. Think of 'expenditure' on education as a form of investment that is justified by the higher productivity and earnings of educated people. The calculations will then give a guide as to what sectors will best 'pay off'. These are the sectors that are to be developed.

It is evident that each of the main approaches to planning has value and each merits exploration. The chief danger to be avoided is to think of any one of the three as being in a sense absolute. In fact, each is only an index, a guide – certainly not an exclusive guide – to the formulation of educational policy. In one sense, they are not even indices of the same thing but rather different views of the nature of education. Is education a consumer good to be valued for its own sake or an investment good to be valued for the contribution that it makes to economic growth, or both? Clearly, the answer to this question will depend on time and place, and economics is only one of the many disciplines that will have to be brought to bear upon the answers. After all, education is not a branch of applied economics. In the end, perhaps educators must have the last word.

This point, we hope, will not be obscured by the fact that three out of four writers in the 1967 Year Book were economists. This is simply a reflection on the current state of affairs: the recent impetus to planning has come from the desire to harness education to economic growth, in consequence of which economists at the moment have the ears of administrators more frequently than sociologists, psychologists or educationists.

National Approaches to Planning

The purpose of the 1967 Year Book was not to present a false front of consensus about the theory and practice of educational planning, but to display a diversity of approaches and examples of a range of activities in different countries. To the student of comparative education this represents a challenge and an invitation to theorize. What factors determine the attitude of a particular society to planning and its readiness to act in accordance with the advice of planners? Are they cultural, social, economic, administrative or political? On the whole, low-income countries have been more active in the field than high-income countries. Many of our articles dealt with Africa, but it proved impossible to obtain an adequate review of planning in Asia.

Why? In part perhaps because the resources of European and American scholarship are now heavily invested in Africa, so that few foreigners can write authoritatively about the experiences of, say, India or Pakistan, while Indian and Pakistani scholars are too busy with the actual work of planning to step back and view it dispassionately.

But the questions remain: why are low-income countries apparently fascinated? Do they see in planning a device for securing rapid development cheaply and easily? Or was the cynic right when he said that planning is easier than governing? In any case, of course, in under-developed countries almost anything that is done to increase the amount of education provided will have good results in the long run. But in the short run?

Why do most highly industrialized countries of the West seem somewhat reluctant to adopt educational planning wholeheartedly? Is it because the patterns are set and rigid, the administration inflexible? Or is it because the task really is too complicated and difficult? And why the differences say between the U.K. and France?

Present Problems

We make no pretence at having covered all the aspects of educational planning, and we are particularly conscious of having neglected problems of administration and implementation: there is much in the 1967 *Year Book* about how to draw up plans but little about how to put them into action. Our excuse is chiefly lack of space. There are, however, a number of important questions to which no assured answers can be given – and they arise whatever approach one chooses. We believe it may be worth while highlighting a few. Thus, should educational planning consist merely of the effort to predict future enrolments and the provision of facilities to accommodate the rising demand? Should one influence the private demand for education to satisfy economic goals such as the equalization of educational opportunities? Are these in fact conflicting goals or could one satisfy them simultaneously? Assuming that economic goals take priority, how can one ensure that education will make a maximum contribution to economic growth? Is it enough to make forecasts of the manpower requirements of a growing economy and to ensure that these requirements will be met by the future output of the educational system? Or must we also relate the economic benefits of educated manpower to the costs of producing them so as to make certain that we have not neglected more profitable alternatives for producing an equal amount of growth? And how are these economic benefits to be measured? Surely, the value of a scientist to an advanced economy consists of more than the goods and services he himself produces? Likewise, how shall we interpret the objective of equal educational opportunities: equality regardless of differences in individual ability or in conformity with ability differences? Should planning take account only of the state sector, or should it cover private education as well, including informal education at home and on-the-job training in industry? Should it be entirely quantitative and concerned only with enrolment figures or should it strive to maximize the quality of education even if this might mean a sacrifice in pupil enrolments? Is the advisability of introducing programmed instruction or closed circuit television the proper domain of educational planners?

Conclusion

Some educationists and administrators have, during the last few years, displayed some weariness, even boredom, with the notion of planning. Reading contributions to a symposium, one of them adapted Samuel Johnson's remark about Thomas Gray and applied it to the whole field – 'He was dull in a new way, and that made many people think him great'. Others have reacted with acidity to the spectacle of plans changed, adapted, abandoned and recast, quoting Bertolt Brecht's:

> Ja, mach nur einen Plan
> Sei nur ein grosses Licht!
> Und mach dann noch' nen zweiten Plan
> Gehn tun sie beide nicht.

Yet, looking at the long list of questions in the preceding paragraphs, may it not be that, in the end, the most valuable contribution of planners, economists and statisticians may prove to be that they obstinately force upon the attention of policy makers the imperative need to take account of factors that might otherwise be overlooked? It is impossible to devote too much care and attention to the development and improvement of education, for nothing is more important.

We may well be grateful for an insistent and continuing demand for clarification coming from a new quarter.

Nor is there any need to be afraid of the influence of economists – or of any other social scientists and technologists – provided only that we maintain abiding trust and faith in ideals properly denoted as educational. It is fitting and proper to run educational systems as efficiently and economically as possible. It is right that they should prepare future citizens for their roles as producers: they need scientific and technological competence. But the question remains as always: how do we provide an excellent education for our children? How can we help to develop the best that is in them? The 1944 English Education Act laid upon the local education authorities the duty '. . . to contribute towards the spiritual, moral, mental, and physical development of the community by securing that efficient education . . . shall be available . . .'. The order of adjectives is significant. The contribution of economists and planners is of value only so far as it helps to achieve the aims. It is the business of educators to determine how far that contribution shall be taken into account.

Part II

C. Arnold Anderson
Mary Jean Bowman

Editors' Note

The following article was sent to each of the contributors to the 1967 *Year Book*. It sets the theme for the whole volume and goes far to explain our intentions. The authors attempt to define educational planning, distinguishing it from mere prediction and forecasting, and to explore the difficulties created by the fact that most educational plans seek simultaneously to satisfy economic, social, and political objectives. In the absence of anything like a generally accepted theory of educational planning, they review the three leading approaches that have characterized educational planning in the last two decades and discuss some 'models' that are now being used by educational planners. The article is a shortened version of one of the same title in *Educational Planning*, D. Adams (ed.) (Syracuse University Press, 1964) and is reprinted here by kind permission of the Editor and the Press.

There is widespread agreement today in academic and governmental circles that public decisions regarding education should be made 'planfully' rather than *ad hoc*. This consensus extends beyond saying that government should be the principal financial support and even beyond saying that administration of education should be centralized in one or a few agencies equivalent to a ministry. It is widely agreed that public decisions regarding education should take into account policies and developments in other sectors of the society and vice versa.

But there is no equally firm agreement on precisely what 'planning' is or should be. Clarity is not aided by recognition among scholars that no government has ever 'really' planned comprehensively, except possibly in wartime. Certainly at present there is nothing like 'the theory of planning' and even less is there 'a theory of educational planning'.

There are, however, theoretical or analytical correlates – systematized analytical propositions – of one versus another approach to economic and educational planning. This paper will outline and comment on some of the main variants of these schemes.

Defining Planning and Educational Planning

The *Oxford English Dictionary*, in one of its meanings, says to plan is 'to devise or design (something to be done, or some action, etc., to be carried out); to arrange beforehand.'

Dror's statement is more definite even though formulated 'for the purposes of administratives sciences':[1]

> the process of preparing
> a set of decisions
> for action in the future,
> directed at achieving goals,
> by optimal means.

There are several key elements common to these or other serviceable formulations. (1) They specify orientation to the future. (2) There is an orientation to action (rather than to such other aims as acquiring knowledge or communicating information). (3) The definitions imply the preparing or designing of something and therefore are in some degree concerned with deliberative endeavours. Prediction as such is not planning, and neither is forecasting or 'foreshadowing'.

The orientation to action implies that planners presume that their plans will be passed upon and, if approved, implemented. However, implementation is not part of planning itself. Thus Dror drew a sharp distinction on this score:

Planning is substantially – and, in most cases, also formally and legally – a process of preparing a set of decisions to be approved and executed by some other organs. Even if the same unit combines planning functions

---

[1] Y. Dror, 'The Planning Process', *International Review of Administrative Sciences*, 29(1): 46–58, 1963, pp. 50–2.

with authority to approve and execute, these are distinct, though inter-dependent, processes which must be kept analytically separate.

   The analytical distinction between planning and approving or implementing is both important and in some ways troublesome. Planning that is effectively oriented to action cannot ignore the means by which plans may be implemented or executed, whether these are merely implicit in the situation and the planning documents or are explicitly specified as part of a plan. A continuing planning process with operational relevance will entail continuous feedbacks of experience, including experience in the implementation (or non-implementation) of prior plans or phrases of plans. Moreover, practising planners may often seek to involve policy-makers in the planning process as a first step in a strategy to ensure implementation; one could even construct a social-political theory of this sort of planning. But to define planning in such a way as to include as an essential component actual acts of implementation may lead to end-less disputes that confuse what is 'really' planning with who does it, or with whether plans are accepted by the policy-making authorities. Similar are the many arguments that confound the idea of what planning is with questions concerning particular varieties of planning and planning situations, such as: how detailed must specifications be to be 'plans'? By what methods must they be made? What are the powers and the instruments of implementation? Since this cluster of issues receives so much attention in the literature, however, some clarifying comments are in order. Most of the discussions revolve around supposed economic planning, but that area is entangled in politico-ideological controversies. Thus, should planning be identi-fied with a command economy in which the actions of each indi-vidual or operating unit are specified by a central authority? In actuality, no such economy has ever existed.

   Is a system planned if a few priority projects or sectors are centrally controlled while other sectors take whatever is left? Does it make a difference whether co-ordination of activities in the remaining sectors is relegated to a market system (Meiji, Japan), or erratically manipulated by a series of *ad hoc* and often mutually inconsistent inducements and 'directives' as in Soviet Russia? What about French 'projective' or 'indicative' planning that combines widespread participation by non-official persons, persuasion, and substantial government investment in key sectors? In Yugoslavia, decentralized decision-making approximates syndicalism, and Dutch planning pays little attention to details while relying heavily on individual and private decisions.

Indeed, is systematic preparing of plans for future action 'planning' when the basic strategies are limited to manipulating a few monetary and fiscal instruments? Or, should we view as planning only the designing of decisions for action that are specified in 'real' rather than in monetary units? It is possible to plan to give people opportunities to plan for themselves and to induce them to do so in ways that enhance collective goals – which was the essence of Benthamism.

Each of the foregoing distinctions is important and must be examined when comparing the theoretical foundation of one approach to planning with another. But it is misleading and logically unsound to distinguish what is from what is not planning in terms of the instruments of control, utilization of real rather than monetary specifications, emphasis upon tactical details rather than broad strategies, or the extent to which plans are executed.

The dictionary definition used the word to 'design' and Dror distinguished between planning and decision making:

> While planning is a kind of decision-making, its specific characteristic in this respect is its dealing with a set of decisions, i.e., a matrix of interdependent and sequential series of systematically related decisions.

The adjective 'sequential' could be troublesome if we were to take it as excluding all endeavours that did not specify action sequences as part of the decision sets, and it may be better to be more permissive so far as sequence specifications are concerned. Dealing with sequences or not in the designing of a plan is then viewed as an important characteristic that distinguishes some planning methods and theoretical frameworks from others. However, the interdependence among a number of related decisions that thus make up a 'set' becomes an integral part of the definition of planning of any kind.

Even when planning is limited in scope to a few priority projects or sectors only (or even to a single project), decisions must be made in sets that have some minimal internal consistency. This distinction between decision-making and planning ('designing') is implicit in most writing on the subject, even when it is not made explicit. In this sense, even if no other, planning is a 'rational' process. Note, however, that the word process must be emphasized. The mutual consistency is one of intent and appropriate rational procedures on the part of the planners; realization of that intent is not an essential ingredient of the definition. At the same time, the specification of intended consistency provides a key link between a definition of planning and a theory of planning.

This element in the definition points to an interesting conclusion in paradoxical form. Dutch economic planning is total economic planning even though it deals with a few parameters only; Soviet planning, which goes into much more detail, is not total economic planning. In Soviet practice priority projects are genuinely planned, with care given to ensure that decisions are mutually consistent, but the *ad hoc* backing and filling with respect to the rest of the economy is not planning by even the broadest definitions. The bounds of a plan, then, are identified by the limits within which mutual consistency is sought, by the scope of the set of decisions. This is quite another matter from the questions of material or financial planning or of the degree of detail considered by the planners. There is a pragmatic connection, however; it is impossible to devise a consistent plan for a whole economy when all quantities are expressed in physical terms.

Finally, there is one element in Dror's definition that we exclude from the definition of planning. This is his specification of decisions directed to achieving goals by 'optimal means'. This optimization clause, even when interpreted merely as an intent (i.e., apart from concrete realization of optimality) would exclude from 'planning' virtually all of the activities that have actually been so labelled. Planning entails exploration and examination of alternatives, and selection among them; but none of these alternatives will be truly 'optimal'. To strive for optimization would be a negation of operationally effective planning as an action-oriented process in a dynamic world. The search is for the best alternative that can be identified or discovered with a reasonable output of time and effort in search and comparison, but this will never be the best in any absolute, truly optimal sense. In practice, planners' decisions come closer to the notion of 'satisficing' than of optimizing behaviour.

Summing up, we are defining planning essentially as Dror did, but without the limiting proviso of optimization. *Planning is the process of preparing a set of decisions for action in the future.* Though it is action oriented, the planning operation is distinct from approval and implementation, neither of which is essential to the definition. Planning is not distinguished from non-planning by the persons doing it. Neither is it identified by how it is done except that mutually conflicting specifications are eliminated. This definition fits 'educational planning' as well as 'economic planning' and it fits any other sectoral or substantive orientation to the planning endeavour.

The Scope and Goals of Educational Planning

We may begin, then, by defining educational planning as 'the process of preparing a set of decisions for future action pertaining to education'. But this is only an initial step towards delineating the theoretical foundations of educational planning.

It is essential in the first instance to distinguish two very different situations. We can – and this is usual – treat educational planning as an adjunct or subhead of general economic planning. Or we can deal with educational planning in its own right, with economic elements taken only as an aspect of it. In the first case educational planning derives from, or more correctly constitutes merely an extension of, manpower planning. This approach reflects an orientation to planning of production and employment, and the goal becomes manpower production. The theoretical foundations of educational planning are then shared with those that underlie manpower planning – provided the latter pays attention to flows and sequences of adjustment and is not restricted to drawing blueprints for target dates. Since educational planning in practice is so often considered mainly in this context, the relations of education and manpower policy will be treated with some care.

When the aims and operations of education are considered in their own right as a focus of planning, the aim can be as manifold and complex as the functions education is expected to perform. Manpower considerations become merely one aspect of educational planning with no necessary priority over other goals. The focus comes to be more on people, less on production of 'human resources'.

G

A Latin American seminar promulgated an ambitious statement of educational planning that could be matched elsewhere:[2]

The overall planning of education is a continuous, systematic process, involving the application and co-ordination of social research methods, and of principles and techniques of education, administration, economics and finance, with the participation and support of the general public in education for the people, with definite aims and in well-defined stages, and to providing everyone with an opportunity of developing his potentialities and making the most effective contribution to the social, cultural and economic development of the country.

As a description of any concrete act of educational planning, that statement has no validity. It is obviously of no use as a definition. Perhaps it was intended only as an idealized statement of what educational planning ought to be; with minor revisions it could serve as a plank in a political platform in many countries. In scope, it encompasses the entire range from planning flows of students, providing buildings and equipment, and training teachers to a detailed working out of curriculum and teaching methods. Cultural and economic, equity and efficiency goals, are all included. Systematic procedure is emphasized: 'a continuous, systematic process' and the 'co-ordination of research methods . . . with definite aims'.

We may interpret the phrase 'application and co-ordination of social research methods, and of principles and techniques of education, administration, economics and finance' to imply application of theories from each of these spheres. But one does wonder just how men with all these assortments of knowledge (and the 'general public' thrown in) are to be integrated into a planning team. Or is the statement intended in fact to include the school principal's planning with respect to assignment of duties of his staff, and the teacher's planning of lesson sequences and homework assignments? Evidently one of the major defects of the statement is that taken literally it would include the total operations of an educational system.

On the other hand, the statement is equally interesting for what it leaves out. There is no mention of the need to analyse the functions of education, and there is no reference to education other than in schools – an omission that is common enough. The statement is representative also in ignoring the aim of developing strategies to

[2] UN, Santiago Conference, 1962, *Overall Planning of Education* (mimeo), pp. 15-16.

encourage innovations in education, including decentralized innovation as well as experiments sponsored by central agencies. And there is
no mention of planning to take account of uncertainties.

Even within the conventional limitations, the quoted statement
provides no suggestion of anything like a theory or logic of planning,
precisely because it attempts to say everything so indiscriminately.
There is no indication that the authors perceived that choices have to
be made rather than just 'co-ordinated'. In other words, we are told
to look systematically in many directions at once, but beyond an
implied requirement of consistency there is no hint of any underlying
rationale of educational planning in all this.

Educational Planning and Social Democratization

A recent Unesco report on educational planning points out the
need for both educational and other capital investments and then
goes on to say that this situation 'requires that their educational
systems shall provide that equality of opportunities which democracy
proclaims'.[3] But this is not a well-founded conclusion; to agree that
widespread schooling is needed for democratic government or that
economic productivity presupposes heavy investment in training
carries no implications whatever about educational equality. Why,
then, does this assumption gain such widespread support?

(1) Equality of educational opportunity has been widely pro-
claimed as a 'universal human right'. At least in form, this faith is set
forth in societies with the most diverse political systems.

(2) Many countries happen to have become independent just when
relative equality in educational opportunity is approaching realization in the nations looked to as models, and these aims are adopted
by governments of new nations.

(3) By an association with the idea of the hoped-for modernized
production, many conclude that equality of opportunity must play
the same part everywhere that it does today in the advanced countries
One would hardly deny that a population will be better prepared for
modern life if half rather than a tenth receive eight years of schooling.
But these resources have alternative uses. There is a wide gap

[3] Unesco, 'Elements of Educational Planning', *Educational Studies and Documents*, No. 45,
1962, p. 5.

between conclusions about motivation and training and decisions about how to dispose of inadequate resources. Modernization requires that education be given a central place, to be sure, but educational policy has to be related to the stage of economic development. Just as absence of industrial conflict is no criterion of labour commitment,[4] so equality of educational opportunity is an equivocal guide to prudent investment policies. Each of the key terms in most discussions on this topic proves to be ambiguous unless it is considered in a context of sequential social change. But there is also an inherent conflict between the ideal of equity and certain other basic values that also play a key part in national development.

Equity versus Efficiency

EQUITY: If a given group, such as rural children, make up 60 per cent of the total population of children and occupy 60 per cent of the places in primary school, we would say there was an equitable distribution. But this is a very crude test, and it is easy to show that each of the four following variants of this rule has different implications for policy.

(a) *An equal amount of education for everyone.* No country has ever adopted such a goal. Moreover, when an educational system approaches this condition beyond the level of compulsory education, qualitative variations begin to be strongly emphasized.

(b) *Schooling sufficient to bring every child to a given standard.* If this norm is formulated weakly, virtually all children can be brought up to a minimum standard; thus the essence of compulsory attendance laws is that no one is to be allowed to lack the basic minimum. (If performance standards, not merely years of attendance, are specified, this will require repeating of grades and remedial teaching.) Persistence in school beyond the minimum prescribed level will then be brought under other norms, setting standards that only a fraction of the children will be expected to attain.

(c) *Education sufficient to permit each person to reach his potential.* Only a wealthy society would try to meet this stipulation in anything like its full implications, for every individual has very great potentials in some direction. Hence the potentials in whose development the society is willing to invest become limited by convention, usually to

---

[4] W. E. Moore and A. E. Feldman, *Labor Commitment and Social Change in Developing Areas*, 1960, p. 17.

the more 'academic' sorts. Educational plans in all countries rest on assumptions, often unexamined, as to which potentials shall be invested in.

(d) *Continued opportunities for schooling so long as gains in learning per input of teaching match some agreed norm.* The norm is usually defined in terms of ambiguous passes on an examination or the judgement that carrying a large number of children into higher grades will be too costly in relation to their predicted learning. 'It just isn't worth while to keep them in school any longer.' When this criterion is examined closely it raises questions about the presumed outcomes of school, questions of learning versus teaching, and choice among various sorts of training.

EFFICIENCY: Whereas equity is a goal or end in each of its variants, efficiency is a rationality concept: to get the most out of the least, whatever the nature of the rewards or ends may be. In its broadest meaning it is thus coterminous with the whole of rational decision theory, but here we are using it in much more limited ways. The first two efficiency criteria listed start from the assumption that learning as such is taken as the goal, and any given total of resources invested in education will then be most 'efficiently' used when the total aggregate of learning is maximized. The first variant is simply another way of expressing the fourth of the criteria listed under equity.

(a) Selection of individuals for further schooling should be based upon how much additional learning can be predicted for one versus another person. Those for whom the greatest increment in learning is predicted will be the first chosen, and so on to the point at which the assigned resources are all taken up. Extending this to include decisions as to how many resources should go into education, we may set a learning-rate cut-off point. It is universally accepted that the number of children capable of profiting from any given kind of training will diminish as the level of schooling rises. Some can learn more than others, and the higher skills do not need to be as plentiful as the lower ones – at least so long as we define education in bookish terms. But it now becomes evident that the equity status of the fourth criterion listed under that head is tenuous. Unless, and perhaps even if, we define education academically this is in fact an efficiency criterion sometimes dressed up in equity clothing. High-level people are needed, few have the potentials, so we concentrate resources on the talented. But to speak of equity in terms of 'talent' is equivocal, with no more intrinsic merit than race or social class or religious orthodoxy. Moreover, the idea of maximizing learning in a generalized formulation tends to become narrowed to refer to learning that will ultimately maximize a man's economic productivity.

(b) Priority should be given to groups or localities where given educational efforts will evoke the largest response in attendance and in demand for further schooling. This is a pragmatic criterion that relies upon demonstrated aspirations and upon the willingness of a population to sacrifice (at least leisure). It takes advantage of the fact that sub-populations displaying the greatest interest in schooling are likely also to have developed relatively favourable environments for learning among their children, and to have acquired and continue to create extra-school learning opportunities that support the school's efforts.

As a crude decision rule this one favours those sub-populations that are already most developed and violates at least some notions about equity – unless we insert a premise about group 'merit'. The criterion becomes much more complex if we specify it further to distinguish the source or agencies responsible for providing the educational resources. So far as central government is concerned, it may then ask: at which points would an introduction or expansion of centrally financed educational endeavour evoke the greatest response in expanded demands for education over and above what would develop in the absence of such an effort? The answer may then be quite different. In no case is this criterion likely to direct substantial investments to the most laggard communities until near-universal schooling is in sight, but this way of specifying the question implies a strategy that will partially resolve the conflicts between equity and efficiency considerations. The generalized form of the criterion tends to be realized by local interests and resources: gradients of interest and ability to support schooling go together, interest corresponding broadly to the gradients of economic development within the country, to the numbers of jobs requiring schooling, and to the willingness of populations to supplement public with private funds. At the same time, local responses to and requests for experimental efforts by the central government in less favoured areas can direct planners to the spots in which further central assistance would bring the greatest results. And where costs of elementary schools are borne in the main by local districts, the central budget will permit more allocation of funds to special schemes to provide facilities for zealous individuals from laggard areas – such as centralized boarding-schools for middle-school or secondary-school pupils.

(c) The third efficiency criterion is explicitly economic, whereas the others were not necessarily so: invest in education where the expected ratio of gains in economic output to costs is highest and extend these investments so long as the economic benefit/cost ratios exceed ratios in alternative uses of resources. In a free market system a crude short-run approximation to this rule tends to hold among individuals. However, as a social planning criterion it requires estimation of public as well as private costs and returns. Also, in its conventional formulations even a socially assessed economic benefit/cost criterion ignores the processes of change and the effects of current investments in education upon future decision alternatives.

Only the second criterion even begins to bring the dynamics of educational and economic developments into focus. On the other hand, demands for schooling can and do sometimes outpace the aggregate development of job opportunities, a fact that does not enter into either of the first two criteria except as they may be modified to take it explicitly into account. It is only this third criterion that in fact specifies the margins at which decisions are made to invest in education or in something else; even the first criterion was oriented to the allocation of given total resources within education, taking the limits of educational effort as quite arbitrarily established. Unfortunately, the marginal social benefit/cost test is difficult to apply in practice, it requires major overhauling before it can be dynamized, and it is only in part compatible with equity norms.

Some Dilemmas of Democratization

The new nations, where we find the greatest enthusiasm for educational planning, must build a resilient policy along with a productive economy. Officials are tempted into politically-based assumptions concerning the pay-off from schooling, impelled also by demands to 'correct' geographic imparities in educational opportunities. But if rapid economic return is given priority, the second efficiency-criterion presumably would be more appropriate. Equity norms would come in to temper decisions based on the efficiency test and also to ensure that a ground is laid for longer-run developments in the presently unpromising areas, and that economic polarization does not become frozen.

Finally, any chosen policy raises troublesome questions about compulsion versus freedom of choice in education. Balancing equity against economic efficiency is easier if a planner can work within given manpower specifications and shut his eyes to the fact that he is rationing qualified individuals out of the kind of schooling they prefer. Such compulsion can be harmonized with equity only by blatant casuistry. Moreover, restriction on free choice of career can have serious effects upon efficiency through its effects upon motivation. It is only in the more advanced societies that equity can be regarded as essential to or even consistent with economic efficiency but societies at every level need to be aware of the risks of controlling individuals' choices of careers by means other than salary structures.

Educational Planning for Production of Manpower

The essential single-mindedness of a manpower-directed approach to educational planning facilitates analysis of its theoretical bases. However, orientation to manpower production does not necessarily imply that educational planning is a part or extension of highly detailed sectoral manpower planning. Models in which only general levels of manpower are specified are also relevant. There are important differences in how human resource development in agencies other than schools is taken into account, if at all. Furthermore, 'rate of return' analysis with its decision criteria might be regarded as a branch of manpower-oriented educational planning, though the methods and presuppositions are very different.

The Logic of Detailed Manpower Planning

The essential ingredients of detailed manpower plans in all of their variants are: (1) specification of the composition of manpower 'needs' or 'requirements' at some future date (or, less often, sequence of dates); (2) specification of manpower availabilities, which includes estimation of losses (by retirement and death) on the one hand, flows of new manpower out of educational institutions on the other; (3) a reconciliation of (1) and (2). Within this context, educational planning becomes the scheduling of flows of human raw material through the educational agencies and out into the economy as various specified kinds of manpower. In a first approximation, at least, the 'educational system' is taken usually to be the school system, and the rest of the human-resource development programme is likely to be planned, if at all, under other sector headings.

A characteristic of detailed manpower planning that must be faced before scrutinizing its theoretical assumptions is the single-valued nature of all its measures, whether of requirements for particular types of manpower or of its availability. There are no prices and no demand or supply schedules in the economic sense. Rather, in Parnes's words, 'the idea of manpower requirements . . . relates to the functional (occupational) composition of employment that will be necessary if certain social and/or economic targets are to be achieved. The concept, in other words, is more a technological than an economic one.' The use[5] of 'technological', which has become common among educational and manpower economists, means simply single-valued quantitative forecasts. It does not in fact escape economic content, however; instead it carries the economic implication of *ex ante* zero demand elasticity; even if we substitute 'highly inelastic' for 'zero', this is a very strong assumption that goes well beyond zero elasticity *ex post* or after arrival at any given point in time. All changes over time in the numbers of men employed at any given skill or occupation are thereby implicitly interpreted as shifts of demands, and changes in pay rates are irrelevant. Parnes puts it as follows:[6]

. . . so long as one grants that manpower considerations are one of the elements that *ought* to influence educational decisions, then all such decisions, if they purport to be rational, involve manpower forecasts, whether or not they are explicitly made. . . . Otherwise, the decision does not make much sense. Thus, the question is not whether forecasts are to be made, but the extent to which they are going to be based on all of the evidence that can be marshalled. If the allocation of resources to education were governed entirely by market forces, the necessity for centralized decisions on such matters would, of course, disappear. Under these circumstances

[5] H. S. Parnes, 'Manpower Analysis in Educational Planning' in H. S. Parnes (ed.), *Planning Education and Social Development*, OECD, 1963. p. 76.

[6] op. cit., p. 75.

the question whether new facilities and personnel for engineering schools should be developed would be the resultant of numerous individual decisions making themselves felt on the market, with each youngster (or his family) presumably making an individual 'forecast' to guide his action. But since no country apparently contemplates this as a serious possibility, governments are unable to escape the responsibility of forecasting.

The second point to be made concerning the manpower forecasts that underlie educational planning is that they do not, or at least should not, purport to be pure unconditional forecasts. That is, they are not so much predictions of what will happen in the manpower fields as indications of what must happen if certain targets for economic growth are to be realized.

Summing up, the detailed manpower-planning approach to educational planning starts off with the proposition that manpower production is the most important function of an educational system, that it is more prudent to estimate future manpower requirements systematically than to guess at them, and that forecasts of manpower needs (however defective) can be accurate enough to be useful guides. It assumes that skill demands are highly inelastic, and infers from this both the necessity for *detailed* manpower planning and a justification for its technological, non-economic techniques. Presumably this is the basis upon which Parnes justifies technological methodology even as he speaks of forecasts made 'as systematic as possible' and 'based on *all* of the evidence that can be marshalled' (italics ours).

Proponents of detailed manpower planning usually argue that a long lead time is needed, and that manpower forecasting for educational planning purposes must therefore have medium to long time horizons. Further, they assume that students (or their parents) are unwise choosers and forecasters and that central authorities must determine (directly or indirectly) the numbers of places in various schools and curricula without regard to prospective students' demands. Deviation from this position is seen as a concession to other, 'social' educational goals.

Pushing back of all these characteristics, we can begin to construct the implicit theoretical framework at the core of the detailed manpower approach to educational planning.

(1) The first assumption has already been explicitly identified – the assumption of *ex ante* near-zero elasticities of demand for skills (*ex ante* near-zero skill substitutabilities).

(2) The period of specialized training in the more critical skills is taken to be long (irrespective of the length of prior general education). It is no accident that proponents of manpower planning refer so often to physicians in illustration of this point. No one assumes that the training period for medicine is typical, though no one would disagree that medical education requires a relatively long lead time. Medicine is also less problematic on the requirements-forecasting side than many other high-level specialities – at least if one does not raise questions about the 'need' for many fully-fledged physicians at all. In the usual case the future requirements for physicians are in large part derived from demographic predictions, their payment is often socialized, and the demand for doctors is comparatively unaffected by changing production technologies.

(3) It is explicitly asserted that a long lead time is required to provide the facilities in plant and personnel needed to train the new cohorts of manpower. This proposition, if true, adds to the time lapse involved in (2), provided that (4) is also applicable.

(4) Production coefficients in the formation of each type of manpower are taken to be highly fixed. In part this is just a particular facet of the assumption of inelastic demands for human skills: inelastic skill substitutabilities among teachers in various curricula and also between teaching and other activities. However, rigid educational production functions would imply also inflexibility in pupil/teacher ratios, in per student allowance of classroom and laboratory space, and so on. Plans often stipulate adjustments on this score, however, especially with regard to teacher/pupil ratios and teacher qualifications at the lower levels of school in underdeveloped countries. Few plans give serious attention to the possibilities of substitution between skill acquisition in schools and by other means.

(5) It is assumed that the pace of change in manpower requirements is both rapid and irregular and/or that there are critical educational decisions entailing large investments that are both indivisible and specialized in their educational uses. Assuming manpower-production goals as predominant, either of these situations will call for unevenly spaced large decisions with relatively long planning horizons. Unless one, or both of these conditions prevails, the relevance of points (3) and (4) to the argument for detailed manpower forecasting well into the future is decidedly weakened. An

even pace of change would allow for feedback adjustments at the margins at which decisions must be made. Hence, there would be little need for looking beyond the period of specialized training itself. Furthermore, if skill demands change relatively smoothly, the presumption against heeding student choices (as a major guide for expanding educational programmes) is greatly weakened. Emphasis upon educational decisions that entail large and indivisible investments is encouraged by two additional circumstances: the tendency to set manpower targets at intervals of several years ahead; and the association of manpower planning with *centralized* educational planning.

(6) Few manpower planners actually claim a high degree of accuracy in their forecasts. In the last analysis, they rest their case for detailed forecasting upon the claim that systematic attempts to forecast are better than no attempts at all. In the background, however, is the belief that with better data and increased knowledge we will be able to identify systematic deterministic relationships between economic development and manpower requirements, even though the sets of requirements at any given economic level will differ with the industry mix. The major part of the manpower-planning efforts in practice have been directed towards finding these coefficients.

Forecasting efforts to date have not been marked by startling success, and the practitioners are becoming more self-critical. Recent discussions in France have raised doubts about the validity of plans and Swedish investigators have identified gross errors of prediction in that country. A recent self-assessment from the Soviet Union reports that there is comparatively little difficulty in projecting manpower requirements in the service industries or in estimating replacement requirements in 'productive industries'. There has been almost no success in projecting changes in skill requirements in the same production industries.[7] These failures are variously attributed to inept implementation (in realizing 'targets') or to inability to identify the pertinent technical coefficients of demand shifts. A few doubters have questioned the underlying assumptions of technological determinism.

[7] V. E. Komarov (compiler), 'Training of Qualified Manpower', (Selections prepared for Unesco *Readings on Education and Economic Development*).

The foregoing assumptions give us a structural model characterized by technologically determined rigidities and inflexibilities in both the formation and the use of human skills, yet at the same time one marked by dynamic and uneven technological change. It is over-simplified in that practitioners will rarely adhere rigorously to the tenets of a logical construct – which is a very fortunate thing. Nevertheless, this model is both the starting-point of detailed manpower planning and a close approximation to the way the planner proceeds right up to the end.

The model has several further implications that should be examined. It puts quite out of consideration any significant market adjustments to re-allocate available manpower among uses, and it automatically diverts practitioners from considering long-term strategies to facilitate more efficient future short-term adjustments in manpower utilization. It slurs over awkward problems of future obsolescence of the skills of today's output of new manpower and evades the question of whether the proposed programmes of training increase that obsolescence. It pays no attention to any systematic efforts to compare costs of human resource formation of one kind or another with the returns to such investments, or to a comparison of costs and returns to human-resource versus other investments. Practising planners of course cannot ignore costs as constraints upon educational expenditures, but that is not an assessment of returns in relation to costs.

The basic assumptions of the model tend also to constrain manpower-oriented educational planning within relatively conventional limits; in particular, there is a tendency to place responsibility for almost the whole of manpower development upon the schools, even when the skills involved are highly specialized. This bias is not inherent in the logic of manpower planning, but it is a likely by-product of the techniques used. Only in a few countries like Japan, where the traditional loci of formal education have been quite different, are educational agencies other than schools likely to receive careful attention. The other exceptions occur where manpower planners are informal and essentially non-methodological in their approach; Harbison is an example.

Manpower planning in its most elaborated and technical variants has been confined to industrially advanced countries, and it is primarily in this context that the logical model we have outlined has evolved. The less-developed countries, it is said, have the greatest need of manpower planning. But it is acknowledged that manpower planning is especially difficult in such economies because of the (hopefully) rapid and unpredictable rate of change in manpower requirements. Obviously one cannot extrapolate forecasts in those countries. Accordingly, there is greater use of comparisons with advanced countries in deriving estimates of demand shifts, and there is more reliance upon informal and unsystematic judgements. (Notice, however, that French manpower planning, with all of its elaborate refinements, also uses informal judgements.)

But let us set aside these problems of forecasting and accept for the moment the assumptions of high degrees of technological determinism. Several undebatable factors differentiate the less from the more developed economies. For one thing, the fifth assumption listed above is highly realistic when applied to a small and underdeveloped nation: the pace of change in manpower requirements must indeed be both rapid and irregular if economic growth is to be significant, *and* (not merely *or*) decisions with respect to the higher levels of education do entail investments that are large relative to total resources (and to existing facilities) and in a major degree indivisible. However, the first approximation of a closed economy in which most manpower requirements will be met by 'home production' is quite inapplicable at precisely those levels of skill to which manpower planning is directed. In addition, the chances are very large that high proportions of the home-produced manpower at the higher levels will emigrate. These conditions substantially alter the context of educational planning even when its dominant orientation is to manpower production, and the most critical decisions are of a very different character.

Tinbergen, Fixed Coefficients, and the 'Transition' Problem

Detailed manpower forecasting, like the detailed economic plans of which it is a part, has been geared to specified target dates, ignoring the paths by which such targets are approached over time. This is partly an accident of history, but it has also been a pragmatic necessity. The tasks of detailed planning are so great as to preclude elaboration of sequences as well – quite aside from the fact that in practice 'plans' have frequently come out of the shop after the period for their implementation has already begun. Development of ever bigger and faster computers and techniques for their use may change this. There is much talk in France at present of remaking four-year target-date plans each year, in an overlapping series that permits feedback corrections along the way, which is a step in the direction of planning sequences. However, it is not the same thing. It does not examine the implications of its own technical coefficients for the path towards target-date plans. Is there in fact an incompatability inherent in the planner's model that was concealed by jumping from the present to a future equilibrium date without considering the path from now to then?

Although Tinbergen and Correa specified manpower requirements by general levels of education only, this is the question to which they directed attention.[8] Their approach is distinctively of the manpower planning type in several respects. Manpower requirements for the non-education sector are derived technologically from assumptions with respect to national income growth rates (as in French detailed manpower planning); factor combinations within the educational system are fixed, and so are educational input/output ratios (teachers, equipment, etc. per pupil year at each educational level). They demonstrated that under such assumptions (which are less restrictive than with more detailed manpower planning) there can be and frequently (typically?) will be problems of 'transition' disequilibria. In other words, there are hidden incompatibilities in any manpower planning methods that disregard the paths by which the economic and educational systems move from the present to a planned future target-date equilibrium.

To the plodding realist who has approached educational planning from the education end to analyse the demography of an educational system, the sequential outcomes of injections at one point or another and the problems of internal bottlenecks (especially in teacher supplies) – following these through in a concrete case without benefit of any particular mathematical or economic model – the tremendous impact of the Tinbergen-Correa contributions upon planning lore and practice must seem puzzling. The realistic plodder knew well

[8] H. Correa and J. Tinbergen, 'Quantitative Adaptation of Education to Accelerated Growth,' *Kyklos* 15(4):776–86, 1962.

enough that there were problems of bottlenecks, that you could not go in straight lines from here to there, and that many compromises had to be made. He may even have followed through the implications of extrapolating from an initial crash programme to expand education in an undeveloped country, and thereby discovered how explosive the statistics could look – and so could the events. At the most such a man is likely to appreciate the Tinbergen-Correa contribution as a rather tidy but limited sort of check-sheet for the inexperienced, and he will certainly want to add to it. The economist who is used to thinking about accelerators, and who will quickly see the conventional accelerator aspect of uneven educational expansion, may not react very differently, especially if he is used to thinking as much in neo-classical as in Keynesian terms. But this is to under-estimate the implications of Tinbergen's work because it ignores the nature of the process by which most of us, and intellectuals in par-ticular, make a bit of progress in our thinking. To comprehend the impact of Tinbergen's work it is necessary to look at it through the eyes of the technicians and theoreticians of manpower and economic planning. Seen in that perspective it forces concern for a new dimen-sion at the logical heart of their work. It is not merely a new and unrealistic sort of planner's gadget that has to be altered almost out of recognition before it will fit – though that is happening too.[9]

The Rate-of-Return Approach

This approach is central to investment-decision theory. Yet it seems to have been anathema to most planners. The weaknesses of the technological determinism that undergirds most manpower planning are by-passed or listed as caveats and then forgotten. Rate-of-return analysis, on the other hand, is typically ignored; planners who do not ignore it are content merely to attack its obvious weak points and then discard it. Nevertheless there is a small group of determined economic theorists and researchers who continue to uphold this approach and who are making efforts to demonstrate its empirical relevance.

Viewing education as investment in human-resource develop-ment (which is also the manpower planners' view), they ask: how are

---

[9] See e.g. G. Williams, 'Planning Models of Educational Requirements for Economic De-velopment as Applied to Greece', in J. Tinbergen *et al.*, *Planning Models of Educational Require-ments for Economic Development*, OECD (mimeo), Sept. 9th, 1963.

we to compare the relative advantage of such investment with other uses of resources? How should investment in one increment to educational endeavour be assessed in relation to another educational programme? The answer must take account of the time path, not merely the timeless sums, of benefits accruing from the one or the other investment. It is the same in essence as the answer to any other comparison among investment alternatives: whichever yields the higher rate-of-return will be chosen. Many of the attacks on this approach miss the mark and fail to recognize that the same objections may be charged equally against the more pervasive methods of manpower planning. Five common criticisms of rate-of-return analysis assert that it:

(1) ignores the non-economic benefits of education. Answer: so does manpower planning.

(2) catches only direct but not indirect economic returns. This is equally true of manpower planners; moreover, the latter do not build any cost estimates into their models and make no attempt to measure even direct economic returns.

(3) assumes pure competition. False; in fact rate-of-return analysis helps spot the monopolistic restrictions and points to where they need correction. By repeating assessments at intervals, it could become an increasingly useful tool for this purpose. (Neither rate-of-return analysis nor manpower-requirement estimates are once-for-all affairs; as a planning device each becomes more useful and interesting as it is repeated.)

(4) is impractical because the necessary data are not available. This argument is circular. The data needed for first approximations are no more difficult to obtain than those normally used in manpower planning; these data are lacking because few people have been interested in their use for planning purposes.

(5) ignores income effects of ability, motivation, and family status that are correlated with schooling. This charge is more awkward to meet especially where comparisons are being made between returns to investment in the formation of physical and of human capital, though the problem is not statistically insurmountable.

Up to this point nothing has been brought forth that strikes at the theoretical foundations upon which rate-of-return comparisons rest as guides for planning. If the foregoing criticisms were all, the rate-of-return approach would win. It provides a rational model, capable of empirical application, for comparing the economic productivity of one versus another investment in educational programmes, and for comparing the productivity of investments in education with those in physical capital. Manpower planning has no such tidy rationale, and is not in fact an optimizing model at all. However, the above criticisms are not all. To them we must add the following:

(6) Rate-of-return analysis does not incorporate systematic assessment of linkages between educational and economic developments over time. Rate-of-return estimates use cross-section age-income data to measure the life income streams associated with one or another level or kind of schooling, but the time patterns used in this way are not historic or development time. Manpower planning, by contrast, takes as its central problem the estimation of growth rates and their implications with respect to manpower 'requirements' at a future date.

(7) It is objected further that central decisions with respect to educational policy necessarily involve lump changes, in scale units too large to justify use of the marginal cost and return measures on which the logic of rate-of-return analysis is founded. This argument is sometimes over-pressed, and we have raised some questions about it earlier in quite another connexion – as part of the discussion of conditions that would call for a long lead time in educational planning (pages 99–100). However, estimates of rates of return at a particular time can at best no more than suggest a direction of change, not a magnitude; to assume that they alone are sufficient to indicate how big a big and discontinuous alteration to the educational system should be is a serious error.

(8) It is objected also that market prices, with or without an 'incomes policy', are faulty indices of the productivity of such people as doctors and nurses, and that administered prices (wages, salaries) in a command economy are not measures of productivity for anyone. A rate-of-return devotee would respond that if and where this is the case one would use shadow prices for both cost and return estimates. But this leaves unanswered the question whether, in such circumstances, it is more practicable to start from quantity or from shadow-price evaluations.

Evidently both manpower planning and rate-of-return approaches have severe limitations. The contrasts between them have roots deep in the ways men look at political-economic systems and in the controls over those systems that are attempted in practice. Matching the insights from such different approaches is not easy. On the other hand, we may find keys to unlock some of the doors if we look more carefully at a question that is politically neutral in itself; the implications of substitution and demand elasticities and inelasticities.

The Importance of Substitution Elasticities

Underlying objections (6) and (7) and even, in part, objection (8) to rate-of-return analysis as a planner's guide, is the assumption of inelasticities all along the line, the technological determinism of manpower planning models. Planning applications of rate-of-return analysis in any formal or routine manner would entail one of the following two choices. One could make correspondingly extreme assumptions of the opposite kind: *ex ante* highly elastic demands for skills and hence high skill substitution elasticities. Or, one could think in terms of the production of human beings, each of whom embodied a large diversity of skills: high flexibility in allocation of *individuals* among jobs, whatever the elasticities of substitution among particular skills.[10] Despite confounding by political ideologies, or perhaps partly because of that, the contrast between the manpower and the rate-of-return protagonists in their assumptions concerning substitution elasticities is at the heart of the dispute.

The National Manpower Council included among its indicators of shortage the desire to hire more men than can be found *at existing prices* and the desire to get better-quality people than are available *at current rates of pay*.[11] In this over-simplified form, these propositions resemble the common view of technicians in that pricing is not introduced as an equilibrator. Conversely, an 'excess' is expressed by unemployment of a skill (not necessarily of the skilled person) at a going rate of pay.

If both supply and demand for skills were in fact highly inelastic, crude counts of men seeking jobs and of job vacancies would give us measures of excess or shortage that would be modified very little by

---

[10] Rigid complementarity between education at school and on-the-job learning is not precluded by the rate-of-return approach.

[11] National Manpower Council, *A Policy for Scientific and Professional Manpower* (New York: Columbia University, 1963), pp. 143–6.

introducing pricing to equilibrate the market. In the short run neither the pricing process nor any other mechanisms available to central planners would be equal to the task. Under such conditions, the way in which shortage and excess are conceived and the way alternatives are compared in the planning process would make very little difference; shortages would in any case reveal themselves in the unemployment of the factor(s), human or physical, with which they are complementary in the production process. Approximations to this sort of extreme situation are sometimes cited to illustrate the limitations of a pricing mechanism to guide decisions and the tendencies (given inelasticities) for over-adjustments to appear, now in one direction and now in the other. Rate-of-return analysis is then alleged to be too delicate an instrument, suitable only for optimizing at fine decision margins but liable to distortion in the big decisions. Such an allegation rests upon a mistaken analogy between hog-cycle phenomena (the cobweb theorem) and the quite different matter of use of rate-of-return analysis as a planner's tool. Nevertheless, to the degree that short-term fixed-factor proportions are approximated in a dynamic setting, we are in trouble. The burden upon planners and market-adjustment mechanisms will become intolerably severe, whatever the models or methods of planning, unless we train individuals capable of doing a variety of things or of learning quickly to do them. For the unquestioned high priority, definitely intra-marginal decisions in a world of high inelasticities and rapid change, rate-of-return analysis is clearly irrelevant. So is overall manpower planning, with its attempted neat fits and consistency tests. This point is often missed in discussions of Soviet practice. Establishment of priority claims on manpower resources to meet the needs (or wants) of favoured projects, as in the Stalinist period in Russia, is not overall manpower planning at all. It is workable only to the extent that there is technical flexibility with respect to utilization of resources, human and non-human, in the left-out, non-priority spheres of life.

Towards Designs for Decision

Decision implies choice,[12] and preparation of a set of decisions implies

---

[12] For a discussion of the dimensions of choice and 'opportunity costs', see M. J. Bowman, 'Costing of Human Resource Development', *The Economics of Education: Proceedings of a Conference of the International Economic Association*, eds. E. A. G. Robinson and J. E. Vaizey (London: Macmillan, 1966).

both tests of internal consistency within the set and (at least informal) consideration of alternative decision sets. As soon as we go beyond the manpower orientation, some of the alternatives will involve choices that shift priorities among the goals of educational planning. These might include, for example, variations of emphasis upon equity versus economic efficiency and alternative compromises to resolve some of the conflicts between them.

Whatever the goal priorities, assessments of benefits forgone, in the broadest sense, are at the core of decision-making.

For whom the choices are made, at whose cost: In economic analysis it is important to consider choices from the viewpoint of a student (or his family) and from that of a business firm that trains its employees. These are essential considerations for the educational planner as well; incentive structures and private behaviour are parameters, elements that he may seek to alter but that also constrain what he can do. Even in a command economy the central planner must take account of private decisions and motivations. However, in this paper we are not dealing with planning by families or firms as such. The 'for whom, at whose cost' dimension centres on the equity-efficiency problem; the educational system both distributes opportunities and sifts out talent in the public interest.

The scale units in which decisions are made and alternatives compared: Comparisons may be made among alternatives that involve only small, marginal shifts in numbers attending college, for example; on the other hand, decisions might involve large proportionate increases in the student body.

When planners' decisions entail smooth and gradual changes only, there can be continuous reassessments and feedback to guide subsequent decisions at the new margins; in such situations we can use measurements that are not suitable when the changes are large, discrete, and non-reversible (because large). In the latter case assessments of alternatives have to be in larger-scale units. It is then essential to distinguish cases in which it would be possible to sum small-unit measures to arrive at totals from cases in which measurements must be in lumped units. This problem arises *ex ante* only; *ex post* aggregations at any level incorporate the working out of interdependencies that would have invalidated simple summation of micro *ex ante* estimates. But planning is an *ex ante* activity. This problem of scale units is a basic point of dispute between most manpower planners and the economists who think in terms of 'rate of return'. Large-unit scale of public action is one of the considerations that underlie the manpower planners' pragmatic use of technologically deterministic models.

The transferability potential: There are important differences between services that are (*a*) in fact marketed, (*b*) potentially marketable, and (*c*) not potentially marketable or even transferable. For the first we have approximate measurements, at least, ready to hand. For the second we can construct cardinal measures, in principle and in practice, to a far greater degree than is usually assumed. The measurement problem is most recalcitrant for the third case: non-transferable benefits achieved or forgone. The case for maximizing individual freedom of choice is greatly strengthened when these non-measurable elements in returns to education are considered. They cannot be systematically planned in any other way, but to ignore them is to create a bias against them in the planning itself.

The time dimensions of benefits achieved and forgone: This involves not merely one as against another date, but comparisons along different time paths. It is a matter not only of the problems of time sequences and internal consistency of plans noted earlier in this paper, but of time preferences also – choices between sacrifices now in order to have more later versus speedier returns at the expense of later and greater ones. These perspectives lead also into consideration of the ways in which present choices condition the range of available future alternatives, which brings us to the fifth and sixth dimensions.

The pace of change: This should not be confused with the problem of lump decisions. This dimension has components that are autonomous and others that are endogenous to the projections made by planners, in several respects. Coefficients used by manpower planners incorporate conditional projections of the pace of change in economic structure and productivity, but this is the superficial side of the picture. The realized pace of change will determine also the pace of skill obsolescence in ways that manpower planning commonly neglects. Lying behind the pace of change are social and political pressure for educational expansion and the momentum that these may build up. Numerous decision problems in educational planning are bound up with adaptations to the pace of change, its speed and unevenness.

The knowledge and uncertainty dimensions of choice: These should be distinguished from problems of measurability related to scale units and the absence of transferabilities. This dimension is associated with the future-oriented nature of planning, the distance of the planning horizon, and the pace of change. Yet it is analytically distinct and carries its own implications for the rationale of planning methods.

The institutional constraints upon decisions: This is a matter of identifying the room for manœuvre in the development of educational plans. Early in this paper we took note of (and set aside as fallacious) the arguments that we have planning only if the planners possess control instruments of the sorts found in 'command economies'. That argument overlooks the fact that the command system also constrains planning; it prohibits the use of instruments of indirect control or direction through manipulation of opportunities and incentives in a market economy.

Paradoxically, perhaps, many economists tend to regard 'economic constraints as 'objective' whereas all other constraints are 'subjective'. This is a gross illogicality that stems from a particular disciplinary perspective. Institutional constraints are not separable into economic, political, and so forth; rather they inevitably inject biases against experimentation outside specified limits, though the direction and degree of these biases differ from one society and situation to another. It is the prevalence of certain institutional constraints that explains why educational planners have given so little explicit attention to designs that would encourage innovative behaviour – including innovation in developing an educational system. Institutional constraints are of course bound up with preconceptions concerning every aspect of education and its relation to society. These preconceptions range, for example, from reified theories of economic progress and development to reified psychological theories of of the nature of human learning, and even to perceptions of what gives a nation 'status' in the world today.

Concerning Shortage and Excess

All the elements in educational decisions can, in principle, be expressed in quantitative terms, whether or not they are easily measurable in practice; more of this versus more of that, more quality versus more people 'put through' classrooms. A conceptual clarification of what is meant by 'shortage' and 'excess' is logically prior to any reasoned attempt at manpower-oriented educational planning.[13] Curiously, this question rarely gets explicit attention, partly because most planners are 'technicians' who ignore the operation of markets as adjustment mechanisms. However, the market economists' identifications of shortage or excess on the basis of a rise or fall in price, or even of a rise or fall relative to incomes in other occupations, are also arbitrary and unsatisfactory. Even within a narrowly economic framework and a market system, such approaches ignore costs (benefits forgone). Rate-of-return analysis has the advantage that it incorporates considerations of cost, whatever its limitations in other respects.

But what about social ends and social benefits that are not incorporated in market measures? The National Manpower Council, among others, attempted to define excess and shortage for a wide variety of situations; it gave up in defeat, summing up with the sound but unhelpful assertion that ultimately 'shortage' and 'excess' are social judgements.[14] We would argue that shortages and excesses are manifestations of past faulty allocations of scarce resources among alternative investments; the allocations are faulty relative to some preferred and feasible (but not necessarily optimal) set of alternatives. Viewed in this way, the estimation of prospective shortage and excess of human skills falls into place as a basis for decisions among human investment alternatives.

Education as a value in itself is included in the analysis, but as an end product, like other end products, to which more or less resources are allocated. The differences do not lie in time perspectives, for consumer returns to education (or political or social returns) may have quite as extended a time horizon as returns associated with increased productivity of 'human resources'. If we take indirect economic effects of the diffusion of schooling into account, even the distinction between investment in formation of a producer's good (human producer capital) and other aspects of returns to education becomes blurred. The critical difference here lies in difficulties of measurement.

---

[13] M. J. Bowman, 'Educational Shortage and Excess', *Canadian Journal of Economics and Political Science* 29(4): 446–61, 1963.

[14] op. cit.

There is every practical reason to begin with the more measurable variables and then extend the analysis to incorporate the less measurable and the unmeasurable.[15]

For and Against Consistency

Early in this paper we stressed consistency within decision-sets as an element in defining what planning is. Consistency tests are an explicit part of manpower planning and of the Tinbergen models. The rate-of-return technique is not planning in this sense; it is only one criterion that would be utilized by astute planners. This difference is more than accidental.

Emphasis upon rate-of-return criteria has been more prevalent among American economists, who would give the market mechanism a larger part of the job of co-ordination. Starting from this more 'open' orientation, a few selected instruments of public policy can be utilized to induce and to guide market processes in the desired direction. At the same time there can be provision also for limited public enterprises and of subsidies for social infra-structure. Consistency in planning could be there in such an open system, but it would work itself out in less visible forms. Certainly consistency is a requisite, if we mean by planning a realistic appraisal of alternatives and of impossibilities and the development of strategies and tactics that are mutually supportive. To be consistent will be to co-ordinate the components of decision-sets to provide order rather than chaos and to reconcile competing ends.

But what about the emphasis upon consistency as we find it represented in formal models of manpower planning? There is a case against, as well as a case for, consistency. When it becomes a planner's fetish, it strengthens biases towards technocratic values. The problem is not that errors of forecasting are so great as to make scrupulous concern with detailed consistency irrelevant. Nor is the objection

<hr/>

[15] Michael Kaser approximates such a procedure in his attempts to analyse social investments. However, he argues for putting all non-market values on the 'benefit' rather than the 'cost' side of the ledger. The arbitrary and narrow definition of costs in such a treatment confuses thinking about the nature of choices and what is forgone and impedes effective treatment of the timing of the cardinally measurable returns to one as against another investment. Nevertheless, he had made a beginning in efforts to include a broad range of ordinal as well as cardinal variables within a systematized planning process. For a recent example of his approach, see his *The Analysis of Costs and Benefits of Social Programs*, prepared for the November 1963 meeting of the European Expert Group on Problems and Methods of Social Planning, Economic Commission for Europe (mimeo). See also M. J. Bowman, 'Costing of Human Resource Development', op cit.

only that this sort of an image of what planning 'should be' has led in the past to patchwork attempts to conceal planning failures. More important is what consistency leaves out. And this brings us back to unmeasured values. Are they pushed outside the realm of choice because they are 'invisible'? How does one then devise a consistent plan that will both stimulate and neatly harness creativity and innovative energy? (Or is the planner by nature suspicious of innovation?) Where do the observed rising productivity coefficients come from, for that matter?

Planning for a dynamic future requires planning for flexibility, both in the human resources we create and in the scope for future revision of plans. It must be evident also that however important the skilled, the planner-technicians, most important of all is men – wise enough not only to plan for others but also to plan so as to encourage others to plan for themselves, whether in a socialist state of a welfare state. In the end, that might prove to be the important guide to educational planning even when economic development is the sole goal. It is assuredly essential if the non-measurables are to be given adequate scope.

BIBLIOGRAPHY

Chesswas, J. D. *Educational Planning and Development in Uganda.* (African Research monographs) Paris, Unesco: International Institute for Educational Planning, 1966. 97 pp.
This is the first in a series of African case studies designed to analyse the major problems of educational planning in developing countries:

integration of economic and educational planning, costing and financing of educational development, the effect of rapid expansion on the quality of education. Other volumes deal with Nigeria, Tanzania, Ivory Coast, Senegal, etc.
Further International Institute of Education Planning publications include a *Bibliography*, and a *Directory of Training and Research Institutions*.

Curle, Adam. *Planning for Education in Pakistan: a Personal Case Study.* London, Tavistock, 1966. xxii, 208 pp.
This is an extensive analysis of the policy developed by the Pakistan Planning Commission for the improvement of education in Pakistan.

Davis, Russel G. *Planning Human Resource Development: Educational Models and Schemata.* Chicago, Rand McNally, 1966. xi, 334 pp.
The following are discussed and illustrated with models and schemata: manpower–education targets for schools and training establishments; the planning of quality education programmes and the estimating of costs; estimating resources available for the implementing of these programmes.

Harbison, Frederick and Myers, Charles A. *Manpower and Education: Country Studies in Economic Development.* (McGraw-Hill series in International Development) New York/London, McGraw-Hill, 1965. xiii, 343 pp.
Thirteen studies of developing countries deal with the effects of manpower and education on economic growth. As such it forms a supplement to the authors' previous book *Education, Manpower and Economic Growth: Strategies of Human Resource Development*, published by McGraw-Hill in 1964.

Internationales Seminar über Bildungsplanung, Berlin, 1966. *Referate und Diskussionen*, Berlin, Institut für Bildungsforschung in der Max-Plank-Gesellschaft, 1967. xxiii, 317 pp.
Papers were delivered by S. B. Robinsohn, F. Edding, Alexander King and others on methodological and applied problems concerning educational planning. Various bibliographies include one of OECD publications.

Lyons, Raymond F. (editor). *Problems and Strategies of Educational Planning: Lessons from Latin America.* Paris, Unesco : International Institute of Educational Planning, 1965. viii, 117 pp.

The Latin American scene is sketched first; accomplishments to date are then described, and finally some major challenges to educational planning are underlined.

OECD *Methods and Statistical Needs for Educational Planning.* Paris, OECD., 1966. 363 pp.

'. . . the purpose of the handbook is to assist OECD member countries in the long-term development of their educational statistics and to provide a basis for the collection of internationally comparable statistics useful to educational planners in OECD member countries.' Methodology of educational planning is also thoroughly examined.

OECD Directorate for Scientific Affairs. *Manpower Forecasting in Educational Planning: Report of the Joint EIP/MRP Meeting.* Paris, December 1965. (Human Resources Development.) Paris, OECD, 1967, 194 pp.

The way in which manpower forecasts are used in educational planning is described from a technological and methodological viewpoint. The balance between 'social demand' for education and 'economic requirements' in various European countries are analysed.

OECD Study Group in the Economics of Education. *Organizational Problems in Planning Educational Development.* Paris, OECD, 1966. 109 pp.

This volume contains the papers presented at a meeting discussing the implications for organization of the link between education and economic growth. Administration, centralization and decentralization receive attention.

Richmond, W. Kenneth. *Educational Planning: Old and New Perspectives.* London, Michael Joseph, 1966. 256 pp.

The book outlines the course of English education since 1926 (Hadow Report) and the 'Victorian Mould' which hampers development, and the developments in education in Czechoslovakia and Hungary since 1945.

Simpson, R. F. *The Methodology of Educational Planning.* Hong Kong, Council for Educational Research, 1966. 36 pp.
This is one of a series of publications dealing with educational planning in Hong Kong and which will later appear under one title as *Perspectives and Priorities in the Planning of Education in Hong Kong* – a *Long-Term Solid-Economic Study.*

Unesco. *An Asian Model of Educational Development: Perspectives for 1965–80.* Paris, Unesco, 1966. 126 pp.
This is a model of a plan extending the Karachi Plan for free and compulsory education of a minimum of seven years' duration to cover all levels of education.

Unesco and International Association of Universities. *Higher Education and Development in South-East Asia.* (The Development of Higher Education.) Paris, Unesco.
Three volumes make up this series: a report by the director of the project; country profiles; high-level manpower for development; and language policy and higher education. Together they constitute a thorough account of the role of higher education institutions in the development of South-East Asian countries.

Vaizey, John and Chesswas, J. D. *The Costing of Educational Plans.* (Fundamentals of Educational Planning, 6) Paris, Unesco: International Institute of Educational Planning, 1967. 63 pp.
One of a series of booklets designed both for the interested novice and for those engaged in the practice and administration of educational planning. All terms are fully explained.

Education Within Industry

from the 1968 World Year Book of Education
Brian Holmes
Laura Goodman Howe
Joseph A. Lauwerys

In the 1968 *Year Book* new ground was broken by concentrating on an aspect and type of education which has been, until recent years, largely ignored by academic educationists. 'The needs of technological and industrializing societies impose the necessity for matching educational output with professional manpower requirements', we wrote in the Introduction to the 1967 volume on 'Educational Planning'. So we look at the education and training provided by enterprises, having regard to the economic and educational histories of the countries concerned, and also endeavouring to bear in mind the philosophical and theoretical questions raised.

The authors in the 1968 *Year Book* show that there are unifying themes in analyses of educational growth in both the developing and industrially advanced nations. The fact that the technological revolution of the mid-twentieth century has raised some closely related problems for the industrialized parts of the world, as well for those nations in the early and middle stages of industrialization, has been obscured by the differences and great variations in technological and industrial development among the *tiers monde* and the industrialized societies.

One such area of concern facing educators and governments in both the 'richer' and 'poorer' nations is the delineation of interests and responsibilities for building sound vocational and technical education and the outlining of spheres of control for this education, i.e. the working out of shared finances, management, etc. All interested groups are attempting to define the nature of education for industrial and developing societies as well as viewing the appropriate roles of industry, the government and the educational system. The discussions in the 1968 *Year Book* search for historical understanding and an explanation of what the interests of the government, economy, the industrial concern are and have been in the education of the worker, the manager, the engineer, and the citizen. Familiar questions form the basic structure of concern: What should be taught? At what levels? By whom? How much can and should be taught in the formal school system, in the place of work? What are the costs and returns? Are the distinctions that are drawn between a narrow definition of vocational and technical education as 'training' and the idea that such education must become broader and teach 'general bodies of skills' meaningful? Some writers point to the interdependence of the state and industry and stress that the latter needs to become increasingly concerned with the role of the schools and with investing in education both within and outside of the formal school system. Conflicts and engagements between public and private education take new shapes and new liaisons form.

Whether the focus is on the vocational-technical curriculum, national policy towards educational change and development, industrial growth and the education of manpower, the questions and insights in the analyses and case studies in the 1968 *Year Book* are relevant to the progress of education in all parts of the world. Examination of the interlocking aspects of education *within* and *for* industry are necessary for answers appropriate to the patterns of development in varied social, political and socio-economic structures.

Background

'As we can learn in detail from a study of the life work of Robert Owen, the germs of the education of the future are to be found in the factory system. This will be an education which, in the case of every child over a certain age, will combine productive labour with instruction and physical culture, not only as a means for increasing social production, but as the only way of producing fully developed human beings.'

Karl Marx wrote this – the date was 1867 – in the course of a discussion criticizing and deploring the decay of the old handicraft apprenticeship. He instanced printing:

'... in former days ... apprentices passed on by degrees from easy to comparatively difficult work. They learned the whole trade, until they were fully equipped as printers. Learning to read and write was an essential part of their craft training. All this has been altered by the introduction of machine printing. It employs two kinds of workers: one grown up, a machine minder, the other, the boys, mostly from eleven to seventeen years of age, whose sole occupation is to spread the sheets of paper under the machine, or take the printed sheets away from it. . . . Many of them are unable to read; and they are, as a rule, little better than savages, quite abnormal creatures. . . . As soon as they get too old for a boy's work . . . they are discharged . . . attempts to find employment . . . in other fields are frustrated by their ignorance, their brutality, their mental and bodily degradation.'

The development of industry during the last hundred years, its greater complexity of organization and its dependence upon scientific technology together with a more sensitive social conscience have altogether changed the picture drawn by Marx and gone some way towards the realization of his hopes about education. To a quite astonishing degree, more and more workers of all kinds, young people and adults, do combine productive labour with instruction, and become 'more fully developed human beings' in consequence. The total amount of 'education within industry' being provided throughout the world grows every year and is already a substantial fraction of the amount provided in school, college and university.

Educational theory has paid comparatively little attention to these developments so that little guidance or advice has been available to direct them into fruitful channels. As a result there are obvious and admitted inadequacies in the training of personnel both in the sphere of practical skills and in the realm of attitudes. The chief cause of this neglect by theorists probably lies in the continuing power of traditions first clearly expressed by Plato. 'When we speak in terms of praise or blame,' says the Athenian in The Laws, 'about the bringing-up of each person, we call one man educated and another uneducated, although the uneducated man may sometimes be very well educated for the calling of a retail trader, or of a captain of a ship, and the like . . . the sort of training which aims at the acquisition of wealth or bodily strength, or mere cleverness apart from intelligence and justice, is mean and illiberal and is not worthy to be called education at all. . . .' In a word, education for virtue and citizenship is good, a view which we can all gladly accept, but technical and technological education is bad, a view we should reject. Our intention, in the 1968 *Year Book*, was not only to gather information from many countries about important and significant new practices but also to direct the attention of educationists to problems of fascinating interest, upon the solution of which depend the prosperity, stability and happiness of modern societies.

Characteristics of Modern Industry

Among the characteristics of highly developed modern industry, which differentiate it from the manufacturing processes of former times, two are particularly important from the standpoint of educational theory. First, occupational skills are very numerous, very specialized, often involve an understanding of science and frequently become obsolete very quickly. Secondly, the social groupings within a factory or a complex as well as the relationships between groups and between groups and individuals are complex, somewhat inflexible and highly structured. Much the same is true of the functional hierarchy.

The attitudes of workers and managers, the training provided for them, the organization of the total process as a human and economic unit, are often very much what they were at an earlier period when skills were fewer and less sophisticated, and when the modes of social control were patriarchal or feudal. Associated with the former stages of development there existed an accepted system which gave to those who had received 'real, genuine education' social status, economic power and political authority, while it relegated those who had received only 'training' – the artisans and manual workers – to positions of marked inferiority. This dichotomy is to be found almost everywhere. It persists where European traditions are indigenous and where they were transplanted during the period of economic expansion and imperialism. Indeed in many colonial territories similar traditions already existed and were simply reinforced when the European trader, soldier, bureaucrat and missionary arrived. Because of all this, industrial and commercial training has usually been considered as of minor educational importance or as the responsibility of industry itself. In many formal systems of education – there are notable exceptions – vocational training finds no place or is reserved for the disadvantaged or less able pupils. At the level of higher education, institutions devoted to technology and professional preparation – other than for the church, law or medicine – are usually accorded a rather low status. Within those universities where technological studies are found, the liberal arts and pure science departments tend to be the most popular and to enjoy higher prestige. Of course, the attractive power of technological studies varies from country to country and from university to university. So, too, do attitudes towards these studies. But even in a country like the U.S.A., where prejudice against professional courses is not very marked, industrialists are likely to affirm that in hiring top executives they are more interested in university graduates with a broad general education than in those with specialized professional training.

At the lower levels of training there is even less doubt. Vocational education at the second level of education does not have the same status among parents, educationists, management or trade unionists as the kind of academic training provided in college preparatory secondary schools. Undoubtedly one reason for this state of affairs is that the academic secondary school system in most countries acts as an agency of selection. A large proportion of its products go on to university and become leaders in politics, economics or social affairs. The advantages to be gained from these highly academic courses are obvious to all. Hence it is easy to see why the French *lycée*, the German, Dutch and Scandinavian *gymnasium*, and the English grammar school have more prestige than do technical or commercial schools.

It is less easy to explain why within any school the so-called practical or vocational subjects usually have little prestige. Some argue that it is difficult or impossible to liberalize vocational studies. Their opponents, following thinkers like Robert Owen, Karl Marx, Georg Kerchensteiner, John Dewey, and Mahatma Gandhi, believe that the basis of a liberating education must be productive work either within the small community, on the farm, in business or in industry. But conviction about the correctness of this view does not necessarily lead to successful practice and the pedagogical problems connected with the provision through vocational studies of a truly liberalizing education are formidable.

Another general feature of the historical situation should be noted. Implicitly at first and then explicitly the rationale for industrial development was the theory of *laissez-faire*. It justified intense competition between different enterprises and between individuals within them. It also led to the argument that industry itself should train its workers and that the aim of this training should be industry's own self-interest. Economic activities depended on the laws of supply and demand. Industrial training could therefore be regarded as the responsibility of industry.

Since the end of World War II, there has been a remarkable shift of opinion in this area. It has come to be generally accepted that skilled manpower is a national resource of an importance equal to, say, developed mineral deposits or oil fields. Hence, vocational and professional training is now considered no longer as current expenditure but as capital investment, an addition to the national capital, just as would be the erection of an automobile factory. Consequently education is seen as one of the most, if not the most, important areas of profitable investment. The economic value of vocational education is recognized, and government spending on this form of education can be justified on national grounds. No longer is training thought to benefit only employers. It benefits all.

This important change of outlook should be considered in the light of institutional structures. The apprenticeship system provided, and in many countries still provides, the main agency of vocational training. It operated chiefly at the managerial and at the craftsman levels. The universities provided, through medicine, the church and law, the administrators of the pre-industrial age. They continued to do so throughout the early period of the industrial revolution. Other leaders, especially of industry, were self-made men with little formal training or education. Hence, historically, managers have been recruited from these two sources – from the universities and from industry.

There are interesting parallels between such recruitment and training of managers and the recruitment and training of ordinary labour. Let us consider the latter. Entry to the occupation or vocation was controlled by members of the appropriate craft or profession and restrictive practices existed then as now. Training was subsequently largely through imitation through the close personal association over a period of years of teacher and taught. The content and method of this training was laid down by members of the union or guild. The balance between practical skill and theoretical knowledge was determined by members of the appropriate group. The young apprentice, as in the ancient Indian caste system, was taken into the master's home where he was taught social behaviour as well as the skill and mystery of his craft. Generally speaking, of course, the pre-industrial worker, like the professional man of his time was not a narrow specialist. He was trained to begin and complete the work of making any item – a piece of furniture, a clock and so on. Similarly, members of the upper groups were expected to perform a wide range of duties. Their skills were for the most part applied to the management of an estate, the church, or an army. Later they were developed in family concerns where owner-manager and worker were one and the same person. Some aspects of the apprenticeship system began to show signs of breaking down when, towards the end of the eighteenth century, industry moved from the home to the factory. In these early factories certain operations began to depend on special skills. There grew up a diversification of function so that the worker undertook limited tasks; the final product being the outcome of work by many persons using a variety of different skills. As this development continued a managerial group emerged which was, for the most part, made up of factory owners. Since those days, the diversification of functions within industry has increased enormously. The gradual simplification of many tasks and the growth of a large unskilled labour force gave rise to the non-craft trade unions, to the need for foremen supervisors and to the growth of specialized managerial functions.

The methods and content of apprenticeship training are no longer appropriate in a highly complex modern industry. Not all industries, however, are complex and modern. The raw-material producing industries have been among the last to introduce machines instead of men. For this reason, in many industries, especially in the less economically developed countries, the proportions of skilled and unskilled workers are very different from those found in a modern industrial complex – say in a Los Angeles oil refinery or, for that matter, in a Saudi Arabian oil field.

In the developing countries basic industries provided the first agencies of vocational training on Western lines: the railways, the mines, the coffee and tea plantations, for the most part employed an apprenticeship system of training. But such a system depended for success on the maintenance of stable techniques and a stable market. It involved, in developed and developing countries, the retention of long periods of training – far in excess of the time needed to learn the appropriate skills. Again, under new conditions it gave rise to abuses. Apprentices became a source of cheap labour. Many were taken on without any form of verbal or written agreement about their training. New industries developed which were not subject to any of the laws relating to apprenticeships. Neither in law nor in practice were the young entrants protected or trained in the way expected.

Problems of Training for Industry

We have tried to indicate the obstacles to the development of a sound theory capable of guiding those responsible for providing training for industry: first, the traditional concepts of a dichotomy between education and training are no longer appropriate. Secondly, the old form of apprenticeship is now inadequate. Thirdly, the traditional conflicts between employers and employed as well as between the industrial and the educational interests have largely vanished, though they still remain powerful as illusions. Finally, even today the necessary role of government in the formulation and implementation of policy for vocational education has not been sufficiently recognized.

Before considering policies pursued in various countries it should be noted that all the above problems find different expression in different parts of the world. In the less developed, of course, the range between newly introduced technology and traditional practice is enormous: the mule and the bulldozer work almost side by side, fields are tilled by camels pulling wooden ploughs or by tractors armed with multiple steel shares. The degree of urbanization, the density and distribution of population, the levels of educational provision vary very greatly from country to country and all these have to be taken into account by policy makers.

Again, the gap between the concepts of education and of training is not equally wide everywhere. In the U.S.A. and in lands with communist government the need to base a sound general education on

vocational training has long been advocated, even though the policy
has often met little success. It should also be noted that the apprenticeship system has disintegrated in varying degrees. Political action in
France almost destroyed it – or at least transformed it – in the late
eighteenth century. In Latin America, too, early nineteenth century
legislation effectively circumscribed the role – never important –
which the craft guilds could play. But, today, the power of the unions
often replaces that of guilds so that they can control recruitment and
dictate the length, content and methods of training. In the U.S.S.R.
their allotted role is to work in partnership with management and
government, and to safeguard the rights and working conditions of
workers. Frequently, where the unions maintain much of their
authority, apprenticeships are unnecessarily long and the content
unduly restricted. Modifications to this form of industrial training
are undoubtedly needed in many countries.

It is probably helpful at this stage to distinguish between agriculture, commerce and manufacturing industry. Developments have
been such that somewhat similar problems arise in the three sectors,
though their severity and magnitude differ. For example, modern
commerce now uses highly complicated machines and computers,
and modern agriculture is turning into a technology, based upon
physics, chemistry and biology, employing skilled motor mechanics
and electricians. So, to a large degree, what is said of manufacturing
industry applies more or less to the other sectors of the economy.

One characteristic of the new mode of production is the extent to
which, at one end of the spectrum, the need is for engineers or technologists whose competence lies in their research, their awareness of
technological improvements and their ability to apply theoretical
principles over a wide range of practical activities. Today the level
of theoretical knowledge needed is far higher than ever before and it
is rising rapidly. There is no doubt that at this top level industry needs
very intelligent men and women with a training equal to or going
beyond that provided in a university in post-graduate programmes.
Whether the universities provide the appropriate environment and
courses of study suitable for engineers is debatable but there is no
doubt that industry competes – and successfully – with the traditional
professions for the most highly gifted scientists and technologists.

At the other end of the scale machine operators perform repetitive, easily learned skills. Between these extremes are workers with a fairly wide range of practical skills and varying levels of theoretical knowledge. What modern industry undoubtedly needs, and knows it needs, is a thorough analysis of the nature of these intermediate skills as well as of those of the two other levels. Evidence from many of the case studies presented in the 1968 *Year Book* indicates that this kind of job analysis is being undertaken in big enterprises. A close and careful linking of educational and training provisions to the many skills required would clearly be helpful. There is the difficulty, of course, that the skills needed by industry change very quickly. This fact does not mean that training need not be provided but only that the programmes should be under constant revision.

Where should the training be provided? Inside the industry or in colleges maintained by educational authorities? It is clear that the costs involved are such that industrialists are not by any means anxious to provide it unless they must, because relevant training is not otherwise available. Instances abound of cases where in former years a large firm ran its own training programmes but now sends its staff to colleges of various kinds or else recruits at a higher level of education than it did. There are certainly advantages in making use of public educational institutions: it is quite likely that the training offered will be more soundly and generously planned and, perhaps, better linked to the general education system. But the range of skills now needed means that very often industry itself can best perform the training: the processes and techniques taught are likely to be more up to date. What would be really helpful would be clearly stated ideas about the way in which training at the various levels of skills should be given inside industry or in colleges, about the manner in which the training should be spread over the years, about in-service training and so on; in a word, what is needed is a soundly worked-out theory of education for industry.

Management and Supervision

Education for industry must include training for supervision and management: and this at every level of the hierarchy. At the top level a distinction may be made between those who are responsible for the formulation of general policy and those who are given the task of implementing it. The possibility of an owner-manager operating successfully becomes more remote as the size of industrial enterprises grows. Directors and executive officers constitute the top echelon of management. There may be overlap of functions between policy formulation and policy execution – but the two are probably sufficiently distinct to call for different forms of training and education.

The political aspects of the kind of society in which modern industry flourishes make it impossible, in fact, to allocate the formulation of policy to one only of the three groups of the hierarchy – the professionals, the technicians, the semi-skilled. Through the trade unions and shop stewards, workers at all levels expect to have some say in the determination of at least some aspects of policy. It is probably anachronistic to maintain that it is the job of management alone to manage. If responsibility for policy in modern industry is widely shared, as is here suggested, then education in the execution of these functions is needed. Whether the same education is appropriate for personnel at the various levels is an open question. Certainly the training of foremen, supervisors and shop stewards involves more than a training in organization skills and personal relations. It seems likely that as the size of the operation grows and the complexity of the organization increases the selection of foremen on the basis of experience and length of service alone will be inappropriate. Here is one area in which promotion policies probably need to be reviewed and retraining policies revised.

Training for responsibility should be viewed against the evident need to create, within an industry or a factory, planning units whose task it is to improve the organization of machinery, assess the market needs, bring together the necessary economic resources and ensure that the products are of the specified quality and completed in accordance with production schedules. Sales outlets have to be planned. In addition, increasing attention has to be given to the provision of after-sale servicing facilities. These operations are complicated by the fact that many industries are not only very large but have an international dimension. Several articles in the 1968 *Year Book* indicated some of the aspects of devising education programmes under these circumstances.

Associated closely with the problems of educating for responsibility are those connected with the inculcation of appropriate social attitudes. These find expression in attitudes towards productivity, occupational and geographical mobility, towards retraining, and towards authority. The feudal and patriarchal system of organization having broken down, new organizations are obviously needed. In many cases these have already been created. What tends not to have changed are the attitudes on which industrial relationships are based. Far too often they are still those of conflict rather than of co-operation, and this is as evident among traditional managers as among old-fashioned trade unionists. Failure at both levels to adjust to the realities of modern industry is an obvious source of weakness. It becomes greater when trade unionists are trained almost exclusively within the trade union, and managers acquire their attitudes within the walls of somewhat ivory-tower universities or through a form of apprenticeship on a board of directors or as executive officers. The need to think out afresh the basis of industrial attitude training is evident.

The Role of Tertiary Education

The type of training needed will, of course, depend on the previous education of recruits. At the technologist-engineer level recruitment is in many cases from the universities or equivalent institutions of higher learning. The particular skills, theoretical knowledge and attitudes acquired in such institutions vary very much from case to case. Industrialists frequently criticize harshly what is provided in institutions of higher learning, saying that much of the content is irrelevant to the work being done in factories and that the attitudes of university men do not result in efficient work. Where knowledge for its own sake is still held in high esteem in universities, fundamental research is regarded as more important than applied research. Moreover, where these traditions are strong the aim of many young students is to become university teachers and researchers, just like their own professors. Doubtless when universities fail to accommodate themselves to the demand for a more practical way of training technologists, attempts are made either by government or industry to set up within the framework or tertiary education new, differently orientated institutions such as the CATs in England during the 1950s and the technical universities in the 1960s. Whether these set a new pattern, or follow the old is interesting. The influence in the U.S.A. of the nineteenth-century land-grant colleges has been to give to tertiary education in that country a more practical-applied emphasis. In England, the nineteenth-century civic universities, though including engineering and other technological subjects, have not been the pace setters in the pattern as a whole, and have not been the prototypes copied by Sussex, York, Lancaster and so on in the recent expansion of university provision. The universities in the Soviet Union retain an interest in pure research which is somewhat different from that in the many technological institutes, numbering some 756 institutions training more than 400 types of specialists. In Japan more than 200,000 students crowd the faculties of engineering.

These institutions of higher education, forming as they do a final and most attractive stage in the educative process, naturally recruit the most able and frequently the most energetic and ambitious students. If they do not provide courses and inculcate attitudes which are relevant to work in industry, the latter will be starved of its quota of high quality personnel. Under such circumstances industry might well have to undertake to provide its own training schemes. The evidence in the 1968 *Year Book*, however, suggests that in most countries industry does rely on institutions of higher learning to provide its top level managers and technologists. General Motors employs some 36,600 college graduates, about 10 per cent of whom hold advanced degrees. Indeed, as Professor Armytage stated in his article, 'industrial firms began intensively to trawl for rather than train, students from the tertiary level'. Money incentives ensure the success, partial though it may be, of this policy. The direct influence which industry has on what is done and how it is done depends upon a wide network of relationships between it and the education sector. Financial support (MIT), consulting arrangements, the release of employees to attend university courses – in the UK, sandwich courses – sponsored scholarships (Alcan Jamaica) and research contracts are some of the ways in which industry co-operates in providing education for higher management and technologists.

If recruitment to managerial and top-level technological positions tends to be from among university graduates, many examples of further training by industry were also given in the 1968 *Year Book*. The system for training for college graduates in the Yawatu Iron and Steel Company involves (for engineers) an orientation course of one week, and an elementary training period of two years on a kind of apprenticeship basis to impart information on staff functions and to train them in scientific methods. Another need is recognized. According to Roger M. Blough 'nearly every major corporation in America is going through a period of self-analysis as to how to improve its orientation programme and initiate training periods from today's college graduates'. The orientation received by the new entrant may be of relatively short duration but, in his own firm, it has a major role to play in 'establishing the college recruit's attitude towards his new work situation'. Tata Steel have a training scheme for graduates which aims at producing metallurgical engineers and giving them a broad outlook on the integrated processes amid departmental inter-dependence in a large steel works.

The National and International Dimension

Firms with international connexions present useful case studies. The main objective of programmes provided by the International Telephone and Telegraph Corporation – with 100 companies in fifty-two countries – is to make sure that the firm's industrial engineers are sensitive to new technological improvements, new methods, machinery and equipment. At Philips International Institute of Technological Studies, postgraduate study for scientists and engineers of all nationalities is provided in electronics – many students have no connection with Philips. This example is illustrative of another trend. Regional schemes are developing to meet the needs of industry. The original aim of the Study and Training Centre for the South-Eastern region of France (CEFSE) was to study the human aspect of industrial problems, but now three broad areas are included in its work, namely (i) the adaptation and improvement of technical skills, (ii) economy organization and management, and (iii) industrial psychosociology. The consequences for industry of rapid technological change have created a demand everywhere for information on planning and the retraining of workers. The International Centre for Research into Vocational Training (CIRF) set up by the International Labour Organization and the Council of Europe collects and analyses information which is put at the disposal of experts.

The trends at this level of industrial education are obvious. Parochialism has little place in the highly competitive world of massive industry and big business. In highly industrial economies there might well be a reversal of Adam Smith's principle of the division of labour which vocational education will have to take into account. Mechanization and automation will, it is claimed, demand high intellectual and moral qualifications and the ability among the leaders of industry to see the *Gestalt* of highly complicated and interacting processes. These demands can be met only by persons who have the qualities of intellect and character which pick them out as potential university graduates and doctoral or post-doctoral research workers. The expense of training such persons is considerable and there seems little doubt that the burden of doing so will not be shouldered exclusively by industry. It is a form of investment in which governments are increasingly interested. To the commitment of most governments to support a national system of universities has been added the need in the interests of economic efficiency and development to build up higher technological education. The emerging patterns of support vary. The extent to which industry is prepared to subsidize tertiary education and make use of what it offers depends on the degree to which existing institutions meet its needs. Where they fail to do so, pressure builds up for new and more responsive institutions where initial, relevant, pre-occupation education will be provided. Industry as such, at this top level, is directly concerned with induction courses, retraining programmes and research. All of them tend to emphasize the inculcation of attitudes which will make it possible for scientists and technologists with good theoretical backgrounds to adapt and apply the principles they have learned to industrial activity. The other focus of interest in all these courses is the development of managerial skills.

The Training of Manual Workers and Technicians

In contrast to this situation are the policies pursued in the training of manual workers as well as skilled technicians and supervisors at the foreman level. Here, differences of opinion tend to be somewhat different in kind from those which are found at the managerial level. The continuing prestige of the college or university preparatory schools dominated the situation. In almost every country such schools take in, at some age or other, the most able students. Thus, more depends on the high quality of their selected students than on the content of the curriculum provided. Consequently, whatever they may have been taught, the products of these schools, particularly those with formal examination successes, are in great demand when they leave school. With this group of students the issues are similar to those described for the tertiary level. Where it comes to a choice between carefully selected young people inappropriately trained but well educated and less able youngsters with a very relevant and perhaps specialized training, the former are usually preferred. The educational content and examination system of the university preparatory schools thus dominate the first and second stages of education.

The issues as far as vocational education is concerned are: (i) should the curriculum of the schools for the less able be similar to that of the schools for the gifted, i.e. general and theoretical, (ii) how closely should the work of vocational schools and the content of vocational studies be related to the needs of industry and commerce? The fact that aspects of the old classical curriculum were well suited to the needs of commerce and the lower echelons of government bureaucrat service complicates these issues by drawing attention away from the problem of devising for less able children a curriculum which will give them at one and the same time a good general education and a preparation for life in a technological society.

The choice in some countries, particularly within the Western European complex, has been based on a willing acceptance by intellectuals of the dichotomy between education and training, together with a proper appreciation of the economic value of the latter. Consequently in the Netherlands and Germany, for example, the functional links between vocational secondary schools and industry, commerce and bureaucracy have been and are close. Schools exist which provide highly specialized courses to prepare students for specific tasks. The levels of technical skill required are matched by the existence of specialist schools, in which the age of recruitment and the length of the courses vary with the occupation prepared for; and by the existence in multi-purpose schools of courses appropriate to the speciality. The close connexion Sir Michael Sadler noted between the nineteenth-century German schools and commercial-industrial life is one of the ways in which the issue of vocational education has been resolved. The English solution is representative of those systems in which little or no vocational training is provided before the end of compulsory schooling and technical subjects are treated in a very general, theoretical manner.

A significant consequence of English policy has been to minimize the influence of industry on education at the secondary level. As a case in point, examinations intended to qualify candidates for various levels of work in industry, evaluate, to a considerable extent, knowledge of technical principles and mathematics. These criteria may or may not be relevant to the future occupation but failure rates – which are very high – suggest either that the tests are inaccurate or that a much smaller percentage of the population is capable of reaching a level of industrial competence than is thought to be necessary for industrial progress. The selection role related to craft union exclusiveness and the testing of basic 'preparation' are confused so that neither is performed satisfactorily. Alternative syllabuses and examinations are not easy to devise, but while control rests with the educationists the approach is likely to remain somewhat irrelevant to the needs of industry.

Faced with this situation, industrialists may be tempted to pursue two policies. First they may recommend that young people leave school at an early age – it is not without significance that English employers have fairly consistently opposed the raising of the school-leaving age. Secondly, they are almost bound to provide in-service training for their manual, semi-skilled workers. Several contributors to the 1968 *Year Book* were of the opinion that industry itself is indeed the place where such workers can be trained best, and many schemes of training within industry were described.

Another situation is found, in Germany for example, where commercial and industrial organizations have a powerful voice in the training of future employees in full-time and part-time educational establishments. The system is based on apprenticeships and part-time vocational schools: the link between these two forms of education is close. At the turn of the century, industrialists themselves established training workshops organized in the same way as actual production shops. The schemes of work are largely specified by the industry for which the apprentice is training. The point of interest here is the extent to which industrialists, commercial and trade organizations determine the form of training even though aspects of it have to be recognized by the federal government.

In France there is a well-developed system of technical education controlled by the state through a directorate of technical education. In this system the share taken by industry remains relatively limited, the role of the particular firm or relevant professional organization being laid down by law. Syllabuses and vocational certificates cover a wide range of occupations at various levels. The role of industry is largely consultative. Individual firms and combines also provide technical education under the terms of various Acts – the Astier Act, the Walter-Paulin and the Debré Acts being among the most important regulations of syllabuses and financial aid.

Communist educational theory closely links true education and vocational studies. Polytechnical education is more than a training in specific skills: it is a way of developing the all-round abilities of individual children, inculcating desirable attitudes to productive life and establishing worthy social and political ideals. Yet communist governments, too, have to face the problems created by tradition and, in practice, the provision through vocational training of a sound liberal education has not been entirely successful. Nevertheless the organization of Soviet technical training reflects a commitment to the need to educate youngsters for modern industry. Attention has been paid to the forms of the division of labour in order to determine their correlation with the types of training that are needed for practical work. In the 1968 *Year Book* an analysis was given in the article by A. A. Vasilyev of the numbers of specialities at each of the levels. Secondary and vocational technical schools undertake the training of technicians and workers. They are very specialized and usually closely in touch with a parent factory. Frequently they produce goods or services for the market. Schools are also located in factories. The description of the training of personnel in the Moscow Light-Car Plant, by M. T. Plyasov, and in the Karl Liebknecht Transformer Works, by Siegfried Berndt, illustrated how attempts are made to provide general and technical education – practical training under specific production conditions in the workshops, and training under normal production conditions. Moreover, the Moscow plant illustrates how attempts are made in the U.S.S.R. to integrate general and vocational education through industry's participation in the training of youngsters still at school in the ninth and tenth forms. If the original intention of the Kruschev reform, which was to set aside in the ninth, tenth and eleventh grades a third of the time for productive work in a factory or on a farm, has not been achieved in practice, recognition of this problem in education as one of the most impoitant in the second half of the twentieth century gives renewed importance to the theories of Kerschensteiner, Dewey and Gandhi.

General Conclusions

In spite of all these differences in national policy, it is evident from the articles in the 1968 Year Book that few informed people consider that the problem of industrial training and education can be solved other than through some kind of partnership between educationists, employers, employees, and public authorities. Legislation throughout the world in recent years indicates the serious view governments now take. The list given on pages 86–87 of the Year Book shows how, in many cases, the law relating to vocational education is embodied in general educational legislation. Special enactments regarding apprenticeships have recently been made in many countries.

The total configuration of interest decides whether or not the voluntary principle can be retained. What is needed, however, is a co-ordinated system of policies at a national level which will deal with vocational guidance, methods of recruitment, the content of pre-occupational training, in-service training, and the examination systems which serve two functions – those of selection and of qualification. The cost of providing such a comprehensive system will be very great. Its success will depend not only on the soundness of the education provided but on the realization that promotion policies, wage and salary schedules, and restrictive practices all play a part. Traditionally the interests of employer and employees have been in conflict. In most countries government has regarded specific vocational training as the responsibility of industry. Educationists, with notable exceptions, have tended to regard industrial training as different from and inferior to true education. Changing circumstances have placed vocational or technical training at all three levels of education, in terms of skills both practical and managerial, in the forefront of the world's educational problems. They are different in developed countries from those found in less developed countries. The gap, however, is probably narrowing and certainly the interchange of personnel between the highly- and the less-industrialized countries makes some appreciation of each other's difficulties and some common basis of education very necessary. The need to extend general education so that managers, technologists, technicians and workers share the same basic knowledge, skills and attitudes is becoming apparent, especially in countries where democratic pressures make collaboration and co-operation an essential prerequisite of economic success.

Practical approaches to a solution of the problems are perhaps less abundant than general and somewhat vague theories. Perhaps the need is greatest for practical and regulating theories which can be given institutional form in educational practice. Curriculum development, the organization of schools inside and outside industry, examinations for vocational competence in a world of changing skills – here are the areas of vital concern to educationists and industrialists alike. It is our hope that the 1968 *Year Book* will help to stimulate more abundant and more vigorous thinking in this immensely promising and important field, a development which would help to draw together the worlds of industry and of education to their mutual benefit and to that of all of us.

BIBLIOGRAPHY

Artz, Frederick B. *The Development of Technical Education in France 1500–1850*. Cambridge (Mass.)/London, The Society for the History of Technology/MIT Press, 1966. x, 274 pp.
This work traces the early developments and final establishment of technical education in France. It has been described as 'the first

comprehensive book on the basic historical background of modern technical education'.

Beveridge, Andrew. *Apprenticeship Now: Notes on the Training of Young Entrants to Industry.* London, Chapman and Hall, 1963. 168 pp.
This book is written 'primarily to help the newly appointed training officer or the executive in the smaller firm faced with the task of installing a training scheme.' Practical information, such as agreements governing training in industry, is included.

Blaug, Mark and others. *The Utilization of Educated Manpower in Industry: a Preliminary Report.* (London School of Economics and Political Science, Unit for Economic and Statistical Studies on Higher Education, Reports No. 2) London, Oliver and Boyd, 1967. ix, 103 pp.
Taking the British electrical engineering industry as an example, the preliminary findings of a large-scale survey of the utilization of educated manpower in industry are presented.

Burt, Samuel M. *Industry and Vocational – Technical Education: a Study of Industry and Education – advisory committees.* New York/London, McGraw-Hill, 1967. xx, 519 pp.
This is a study in depth of industrial involvement in vocational and technical training in the United States. Important analyses of the legal framework are given.

CIRF. *European Apprenticeship: Effects of Educational, Social and Technical Development on Apprentice Training Practices in Eight Countries.* (CIRF monographs, Volume 1, No. 2.) Geneva, CIRF Publications, 1966. 276 pp.
The ILO undertook this detailed study of the history and current state of apprenticeship in eight European countries, covering organization, administration, finance, etc., and concluding with suggestions for modifying existing systems.

Liepmann, Kate. *Apprenticeship: An Inquiry into its Adequacy under Modern Conditions.* (International Library of Sociology and Social

Reconstruction) London, Routledge and Kegan Paul, 1960. x, 204 pp.
This is an investigation into the question of whether or not apprenticeship is adequately adapted to modern conditions. The author argues that the state should take prime responsibility for training for industry.

Perry, P. J. C. *The BACIE Bibliography of Publications in the Field of Education and Training in Commerce and Industry*. London, BACIE, (1963 and 1968). 100/232 pp.
Very concise annotations are supplied.

Shapovalenko, S. G. (editor). *Polytechnical Education in the U.S.S.R.* (Monographs on Education – III) Paris, Unesco, 1963. 433 pp.
The 1958 reforms of education in the U.S.S.R. are discussed especially with relation to the introduction of vocational training into the last three grades of secondary schooling, and the broadening of the scope of polytechnical education. The volume concludes with an extensive bibliography on polytechnical education in the U.S.S.R.

Sivaraman, V. and Mahabal, S. B. *Reports on the Training of Members and Staff of Co-operative Organizations in some Foreign Countries*. Bombay, Reserve Bank of India, 1963. 140 pp.
In preparation for the planning and organizing of the training of staff for Co-operative Departments and Institutions in India, this team reported on trends in the type of training in Britain, Canada, Denmark, Finland, France, Italy, Sweden, U.S.A. and West Germany.

Unesco and International Labour Office. *Technical and Vocational Education and Training: Recommendations by Unesco and the ILO*. Paris, Unesco/ILO, 1964. 36 pp.
The recommendations cover both technical and vocational education, and, vocational training.

Venables, P. F. R. *Sandwich Courses for Training Technologists and Technicians*. London, Max Parrish, 1959. 160 pp.
An investigation into the setting up of the system in which college study and industrial training alternates to provide both scientific grounding and practical experience.

Venables, P. F. R. and Williams, W. J. *The Smaller Firm and Technical Education*. London, Max Parrish, 1961. 223 pp.
This work researches into the special needs of the small concerns in technical-industrial training. Schemes both within the concerns and outside are considered.

Wellens, John. *Education and Training in Industry*. Manchester, Columbine Press, 1955. x, 142 pp.
The three aims of the book are: to indicate current practice; to explain the doctrine of integrated training; and to show that effective training is possible only within an organizational framework allowing for and promoting efficiency.

Warren, Hugh. *Vocational and Technical Education: A Comparative Study of Present Practice and Future Trends in Ten Countries*. (Monographs on Education – VI) Paris, Unesco, 1967. 222 pp.
This study deals with the provision for and practice of technical education in ten countries which have extensive relevant experience. The training of skilled workers and technicians, and higher technological education are dealt with separately.

Williams, Gertrude. *Apprenticeship in Europe: The Lesson for Britain*. London, Chapman and Hall 1963, ix, 208 pp.
As the basis for a blueprint for the total revision of apprenticeship in Britain in order to overcome the critical shortage of skilled labour, the training systems of the major industrial countries of Europe are investigated.

Williams, Gertrude. *Recruitment to Skilled Trades*. (International Library of Sociology and Social Reconstruction) London, Routledge and Kegan Paul, 1957, 216 pp.
In order to answer the questions: what are the reasons for the continuing shortage of skilled workers? How could the shortage be reduced? The factual situation in industry must be investigated, including the way in which people within industry look at training.